COMPUTER ASSISTED LEARNING IN PHYSICS EDUCATION

COMPUTER ASSISTED LEARNING IN PHYSICS EDUCATION

Edited by
ALFRED BORK

PERGAMON PRESS
OXFORD · NEW YORK · TORONTO · SYDNEY · PARIS · FRANKFURT

U.K.	Pergamon Press Ltd., Headington Hill Hall, Oxford OX3 0BW, England
U.S.A.	Pergamon Press Inc., Maxwell House, Fairview Park, Elmsford, New York 10523, U.S.A.
CANADA	Pergamon of Canada, Suite 104, 150 Consumers Road, Willowdale, Ontario M2J 1P9, Canada
AUSTRALIA	Pergamon Press (Aust.) Pty. Ltd., P.O. Box 544, Potts Point, N.S.W. 2011, Australia
FRANCE	Pergamon Press SARL, 24 rue des Ecoles, 75240 Paris, Cedex 05, France
FEDERAL REPUBLIC OF GERMANY	Pergamon Press GmbH, 6242 Kronberg-Taunus, Hammerweg 6, Federal Republic of Germany

First edition 1980

British Library Cataloguing in Publication Data

Computer assisted learning in physics education.
1. Physics - Computer-assisted instruction
I. Bork, Alfred
530'.07'8   QC30   80-41129
ISBN 0-08-025812-3

Published as Volume 4, Number 1, of the journal *Computers & Education* and supplied to subscribers as part of their subscription. Also available to non-subscribers.

Printed in Great Britain by A. Wheaton & Co. Ltd., Exeter

PREFACE

This publication concerns the use of computers in learning physics. With the exception of the papers about CONDUIT, all the papers report on major current work. The CONDUIT paper describes the most successful present distribution method, with particular reference to physics. All of the papers were written specifically for this publication.

No attempt has been made to maintain a *single* position about how computers should aid physics students. Rather, the projects represent a healthy plurality of approaches and philosophical positions. We should resist premature decisions about the role of the computer in the learning process. We still have much to learn, and so experimentation in a variety of directions is highly desirable.

It is not possible to include all the interesting work in physics in a single publication. So this selection should be regarded as only a partial story, a segment of what is happening. The reader is referred to the Proceedings of various conferences for a broader view of computers in physics instruction; of particular interest is the annual Conference on Computers in the Undergraduate Curriculum (now the National Educational Computing Conference).

The individual authors will, I believe, welcome correspondence about their activities.

Educational Technology Center
Physics Department
University of California
Irvine, CA 92717, U.S.A.

ALFRED BORK

CONTENTS

LIST OF CONTRIBUTORS

H. E. BERGESON
Department of Physics
University of Utah
Salt Lake City
UT 84112
U.S.A.

A. BORK
Educational Technology Center
Department of Physics
University of California
Irvine
CA 92717
U.S.A.

J. HARRIS
Educational Computing Section
Chelsea College
Pulton Place
London SW6 5PR
U.K.

D. KANE
University of Illinois
Central Receiving Station
1609 South Oak Street
Champaign
IL 61820
U.S.A.

R. LEWIS
Educational Computing Section
Chelsea College
Pulton Place
London SW6 5PR
U.K.

G. W. MASON
Brigham Young University
Provo
UT 84602
U.S.A.

W. D. OHLSEN
Department of Physics
University of Utah
Salt Lake City
UT 84112
U.S.A.

H. J. PETERS
CONDUIT
University of Iowa
Iowa
IA 52242
U.S.A.

A. A. DISESSA
D.S.R.E. 20C-105
M.I.T.
Cambridge
MA 02139
U.S.A.

B. SHERWOOD
University of Illinois
Central Receiving Station
1609 South Oak Street
Champaign
IL 61820
U.S.A.

K. WOOD
Department of Physics
University of Utah
Salt Lake City
UT 84112
U.S.A.

Comput. & Educ., Vol. 4, pp. 1 to 9
Pergamon Press Ltd 1980. Printed in Great Britain

THE CONDUIT SERIES IN PHYSICS

H. J. PETERS

University of Iowa

CONDUIT has not developed computer-based materials for physics instruction. Rather, we review, test and distribute materials developed by others. In this article we will briefly describe our review process, and tell about some of the materials that have emerged from this process and are now in wide distribution. We presently offer eight such packages (see Fig. 1) and expect to double that number within the next two years. In the past three years we have distributed more than 600 physics packages to hundreds of colleges and universities in the U.S. and more than a dozen other countries.

CONDUIT began as an experiment in the transfer of instructional computing materials from one institution to another and has evolved into an organization that reviews, tests, packages and distributes these materials. The experiment identified a number of problems that have prevented successful transfer in the past: non-standard, system-specific program code, missing or inadequate documentation for the student, and little or no information for the instructor as to how to integrate the materials into a course. For the materials that we now distribute, CONDUIT applies standards to deal with such deficiencies and this has resulted in a number of fundamental choices that have affected the types of materials that we select for review and distribution. These standards have an important bearing on our series in physics, affecting both the current content and the selection of future materials.

CONDUIT Registry #	Package Title	Topic(s)
PHY003	Using Computers in Physics	(Many)
PHY006	Quantum Mechanics	Schrodinger's equation
PHY053	Introductory Computer-Based Mechanics I	Simple harmonic oscillator
PHY057	Mechanics	Newton's Second Law
PHY092	Introductory Computer-Based Mechanics II	Newton's Second Law (two dimensions)
PHY129	SCATTER	Particle scattering
PHY130	NEWTON	Satellite orbits
PHY183	INTERP	Two-slit diffraction

Fig. 1. Materials in the CONDUIT physics series.

GENERAL CRITERIA

First of all we seek *quality* materials. Transfer is of no interest if the materials are mediocre in the first place. Quality is of course difficult to define, but we have found that we can rely on an operational definition: if materials are judged by our peer review panels to be substantively correct and of evident educational effectiveness in the reviewers' opinions, then we consider that the requisite quality is present.

To insure some comparability in reviews, we provide our reviewers with a standard review rating form developed and tested by CONDUIT to verify its reliability. Excerpts from the form are shown in Figs 2 and 3. Our CONDUIT Series Editor for Physics, Alfred Bork, uses several reviews for any given package as a basis for preparing a summary assessment, which is the most important determinant in the CONDUIT staff's decision as to whether to proceed with packaging and distributing a given set of materials.

Besides overall quality, our other principal general criterion is that materials be widely transferable. Both we and our supporting agencies would like our efforts to have maximal impact. This criterion of transferability has led to considerable controversy, especially as it has dictated our choice of programming languages.

PART II:
EVALUATION

Column 1:

Rate this package on each of the selected characteristics listed below by circling the appropriate number. Please complete this entire column before working on column 2.

Column 2:

Indicate the importance of each feature for this instructional package. Circle the appropriate number.

6 Exceptional
 5 Very good
  4 Good
   3 Fair
    2 Poor
     1 Very Poor
      A Item not applicable
       B Insufficient information, can't evaluate
        C Not qualified to evaluate

											Critical	Important	Optional	Inappropriate
A. SUBSTANTIVE CONTENT														
6 5 4 3 2 1	A B C	1.	Definition of key concepts								4	3	2	1
6 5 4 3 2 1	A B C	2.	Discussion of underlying assumptions								4	3	2	1
6 5 4 3 2 1	A B C	3.	Validity of principles, theories								4	3	2	1
6 5 4 3 2 1	A B C	4.	Discussion of relevant literature								4	3	2	1
6 5 4 3 2 1	A B C	5.	Overall substantive content quality								4	3	2	1
B. DOCUMENTATION/TEXTUAL MATERIALS														
6 5 4 3 2 1	A B C	1.	Clarity of information in textual materials								4	3	2	1
6 5 4 3 2 1	A B C	2.	Completeness of instructor guides								4	3	2	1
6 5 4 3 2 1	A B C	3.	Adequacy of instructions for operating programs								4	3	2	1
6 5 4 3 2 1	A B C	4.	Overall quality of documentation								4	3	2	1
C. SUPPORT OF THE TEACHING PROCESS														
6 5 4 3 2 1	A B C	1.	Ease of integration with course procedures								4	3	2	1
6 5 4 3 2 1	A B C	2.	Potential for improving instructor's ability to communicate principles and theories								4	3	2	1
6 5 4 3 2 1	A B C	3.	Potential for improving instructor's ability to communicate methods and techniques								4	3	2	1
6 5 4 3 2 1	A B C	4.	Potential for teaching how to interpret and apply results								4	3	2	1
6 5 4 3 2 1	A B C	5.	Overall instructional quality								4	3	2	1
D. STIMULATION OF STUDENT INTEREST														
6 5 4 3 2 1	A B C	1.	Potential for capturing student interest								4	3	2	1
6 5 4 3 2 1	A B C	2.	Challenge to student creativity								4	3	2	1
6 5 4 3 2 1	A B C	3.	Student choice in patterns of use								4	3	2	1
6 5 4 3 2 1	A B C	4.	Appropriateness for student-initiated work								4	3	2	1
6 5 4 3 2 1	A B C	5.	Overall contribution to student motivation								4	3	2	1
E. COMPUTER TECHNIQUES/MATERIALS														
6 5 4 3 2 1	A B C	1.	Soundness of computer programming methods								4	3	2	1
6 5 4 3 2 1	A B C	2.	Completeness of technical documentation								4	3	2	1
6 5 4 3 2 1	A B C	3.	Portability (machine-independence of computer program)								4	3	2	1
6 5 4 3 2 1	A B C	4.	Ease of program use								4	3	2	1
6 5 4 3 2 1	A B C	5	Overall quality of computer techniques								4	3	2	1
6 5 4 3 2 1	A B C		OVERALL EVALUATION OF PACKAGE								4	3	2	1

Fig. 2. Section II of the CONDUIT review rating form.

PROGRAMMING LANGUAGE

We currently distribute materials in two different languages: FORTRAN and BASIC. The choice of FORTRAN was easy; this is the most commonly used language in the sciences and an ANSI standard has existed since 1966. Adherence to this standard assures authors that their materials will be usable on most computer systems supporting FORTRAN. Standards for BASIC have been slower in coming and widely varying dialects abound. Nevertheless we have been able to define a minimal subset of BASIC that suffices for many instructional programming applications and yet does assure wide transferability.

In many respects these language choices have served quite well. This is especially true in those cases where the student need not get into the details of the code at all, as with most tutorial dialogs and

---

PART III:
SUMMARY ASSESSMENTS

Please comment freely about your assessment of this package.

1. How central is the subject matter of this package to your field?

    ___ critical, absolutely essential
    ___ important to include
    ___ optional, appropriate but not essential
    ___ trivial, not important

    Comment:

2. Is it reasonable to use the computer with this package?

    ___ yes
    ___ no
    ___ not sure

    Comment:

3. Do you recommend the use of this package?

    ___ strongly recommend
    ___ recommend
    ___ recommend subject to improvements (state on next question)
    ___ do not recommend
    ___ Why? (Identify strengths and weaknesses):

4. What improvements do you recommend to the substance, program or documentation of this package, if any?

PART VI

SUMMARY

Please provide a written summary of your general assessment of the package. Your summary should elaborate your evaluation of the substantive aspects of the material.

Fig. 3. Section III of the CONDUIT review rating form

many simulations in which the program is treated much as a black box. In these cases the language in which the instruction is delivered is really quite irrelevant to the student. (It may however be quite relevant to the author of the materials. We have dealt with some materials that were created in a specialized 'CAI authoring language' that was specific to one vendor's computer system. The materials received very strong reviews so we took the effort to translate them into BASIC, with the result then that the author had all the advantages of ease of development and the materials in their final form are widely transferable.)

For some other types of materials, standard FORTRAN and BASIC leave a lot to be desired. The deficiencies arise when the student must do some programming either writing programs from scratch or modifying existing code. BASIC and FORTRAN do not lend themselves readily to structured programming techniques, and we feel that these techniques are especially important for student programmers to be acquiring from the start.

Another issue is ease of modification. At CONDUIT we have felt that even high quality materials will probably be most effectively used by others as *starting points* for developing materials more suited to local needs. This makes ease of modification paramount. There is no question that well-structured programs are the easiest to modify, so again FORTRAN and BASIC are found wanting. And we should point out that this objection applies to essentially *all* types of materials.

We are remaining alert, then, to other potential languages to adopt as CONDUIT standards. The relative newcomer PASCAL has some attraction, in that it was designed in the beginning with structured programming in mind, and it shows some promise of becoming widely enough available to support widespread transfer of materials. But at this writing no commitments have been made to languages other than FORTRAN and BASIC.

DOCUMENTATION

For ease of modification by either student or instructor, as discussed above, and for helping the student simply to understand how the program accomplishes its task, it is important that the program be well documented, and the best place is within the program itself. A good example of documentation that will be helpful to the student is shown in Fig. 4, which is taken from CONDUIT's package PHY003 *Using Computers in Physics*.

In addition to the internal documentation, transferability requires for most programs that the student be supplied with a printed guide that gives background, explains how to use the program, and provides exercises.

Similarly, most programs will require a teacher's guide that states the objectives of the unit, covers theoretical background, explains the algorithms employed in the program, and suggests ways in which the materials can most effectively be integrated into typical courses.

```
1DFMABAS
 10 LET Y=100 ⎱ Initialization
 20 LET V=5   ⎰
 30 LET D=.02       Time step, Δt
 40 LET A=-9.8      Acceleration
 50 IF T>0 THEN 80  ⎫
 60 LET V=V+A*D/2   ⎬Initial half-step
 70 GOTO 90         ⎭
 80 LET V=V+A*D    New velocity
 90 LET Y=Y+V*D    New position
100 LET T=T+D      New time
110 LET D0=D0+D             ⎫
120 LET D0<.2 THEN 150 ⎱   Print
130 LET D0=0           ⎰   group
140 PRINT T,Y              ⎭
150 IF T<5 THEN 40      Return for next Δt step
160 END
```

Fig. 4. An example of program documentation for the student.

WHAT THE SERIES COVERS

Many writers have described the multitudinous ways in which computers can be used in support of learning physics. CONDUIT's present series has examples of several different approaches but by no means all of them. Probably the most significant omissions are direct laboratory use of computers in conjunction with experiments on one end of the spectrum, and tutorial dialogs or drills, toward the other end. Better represented are problem solving, simulation, and modeling.

SIMULATIONS

Three packages in CONDUIT's physics series were developed in the U.K. as part of the Chelsea Science Simulation Project (CSSP). That project is described elsewhere in this issue, as well as are some of the physics materials, specifically. Nevertheless we will describe one of these units from our perspective.

In many ways these CSSP units ideally represent what we like to see in computer-based instructional materials. The programs are written in minimal, transferable BASIC and are well enough documented that instructors should have little difficulty adding their own modifications. The accompanying guides for students and instructors are thorough and handsomely produced. (The latter point is not as trivial as it might appear—more than one student has been 'turned off' by hard-to-read, unattractively laid-out printed matter that so frequently accompanies computer-based materials.)

PHY083, *INTERP*, is representative of the CSSP units. It simulates two-slit diffraction experiments. The sample student interaction shown in Fig. 5 serves to introduce the unit.

As with most instructional simulations, *INTERP* is intended as an extension of the student's laboratory work, allowing essentially as many experiments with varied parameters as the student desires, swiftly and with little effort. The student can thus acquire a broad range of experience with simulated diffraction phenomena in a brief span of time.

```
SET EXPERIMENTAL CONDITIONS
SOURCE SEPARATION ? .5E-3
WAVELENGTH ? .55E-6
OUTPUT INTENSITY PARALLEL (1) OR NORMAL (2) TO LINE OF SOURCES ? 1

DISTANCE TO SCREEN ? 1
DISTANCE STEP   ? .1E-3

SIMULATION WILL RUN WITH CONDITIONS AS ABOVE

DISTANCE FROM        INTENSITY
CENTRE OF PATTERN
 0                   100
 .0001               92.1
 .0002               70.8
 .0003               42.9
 .0004               17.3
 .0005               2
 .0006               2
 .0007               17.3
 .0008               42.9
 .0009               70.8
MORE RESULTS ? YES
```

Fig. 5. Sample student interaction for *INTERP*.

Unlike some computer-based educational simulations we have seen, the *INTERP* package calls students' attention to the nature of the underlying models, and to how the behavior of the models compares with actual experiments carred out in the laboratory. It appears to us that students will therefore come away from *INTERP* with a better understanding of diffraction models in addition to a broader experience with diffraction phenomena.

Another way in which *INTERP* differs from other educational simulations is that the *INTERP* student guide poses a number of questions and suggested exercises that help guide the student

> **Q8** Does the computer produce reasonable results — i.e. what you would have expected?
> You might care to make a scale drawing, or a calculation, to check that the path difference, for say the second or third maximum, is exactly 1 or 2 wavelengths.
> Does this model predict that the maxima are equally spaced, and all of the same intensity?

•
•
•

> **Q9** In what way(s) are the results of Investigation 1 and 2 similar, and in what way(s) are they different?

> **Q10** Now look at photograph 1 which shows the interference pattern formed when light passes through two slits (Young's experiment). Does it have features which are better represented by Investigation 2 than by Investigation 1?

Fig. 6. Sample questions from the student notes for *INTERP*.

through the initial experience with the simulation. (See Fig. 6 for some illustrative questions.) Too often, other educational simulations have left students on their own, saying in effect, 'here's a simulation of such and such physical phenomenon, run it a few times to get some experience in this area.' For a few highly motivated students this approach may suffice, but for most it will not.

PROBLEM SOLVING

When students use a computer to 'solve problems', they may utilize existing programs (e.g., for statistical analysis), they may write their own programs, or they may start with some example programs and make modifications to meet their specific needs. This third approach is used almost exclusively in CONDUIT's problem solving packages. Figure 7 illustrates this with a sample page from the student guide for PHY092, *ICBM II*.

Motion with Two Force Centers

Sophisticated and very interesting motions can be studied by means of this simple, computer-based, iterative calculation. One example of motion which cannot be studied analytically but can easily be studied by the computer-based method is the motion of a satellite under the influence of more than one gravitational force center. The simplest such case would be a satellite in the vicinity of two fixed, equal mass gravitational force centers. Consider such a two-force center system with the (fixed) force centers at (2,0) and (-2,0). The same iterative program applies with the accelerations

An algorithm and sample programs have been introduced earlier.

$$a_1 = \frac{-(X_1-2)}{R} - \frac{(X_1+2)}{R_1} \qquad R = ((X_1-2)^2 + X_2{}^2)^{1.5}$$

$$a_2 = -\frac{X_2}{R} - \frac{X_2}{R_1} \qquad R_1 = ((X_1+2)^2 + X_2{}^2)^{1.5}$$

The students have been led through a sequence of earlier exercises with simpler expression for the acceleration.

After inserting these accelerations into the programs, you can study any number of initial conditions. The motion is, in general, very complicated, but, by using symmetries and lots of patience, some closed (or almost closed) orbits can occur.

Now they are to incorporate these new acceleration expressions into the existing program in an analogous way.

Exercise 30: Investigate the orbit obtained with two fixed force centers with the following initial conditions:

masses = 1, $\vec{r}$=(3,0), $\vec{v}$=(0,1.1).

See if you can change this into a closed orbit by making a slight change in the x2 component of velocity.

A series of specific exercises of the type shown here are posed and gradually the student is led to more open-ended pursuits.

Exercise 31: Elliptical motion is still possible with two fixed force centers! Speculate as to how this could happen,

Fig. 7. Excerpt from the student manual for *ICBM II*.

ICBM II, together with its companion PHY053, *ICBM I*, epitomize the *simplicity* and the *power* of applying the computer to the solution of problems in physics. They focus on the application of Newton's Second Law of Motion to the simple harmonic oscillator (*ICBM I*) and then to the motion of particles in two dimensions, under the influence of a uniform gravitational field or one or more discrete force centers (*ICBM II*).

Those of us who learned our physics before the computer age (which includes the author and probably a majority of the readers of this article) recall the power promised by the universality attributed to Newton's Second Law and our frustration when we found that we could practically apply it only to very simplified problems—the all-too-familiar blocks on inclined planes or weights suspended from pulleys. The computer offers a dramatic change, as the two *ICBM* modules illustrate.

ICBM I and *II* use the now common technique of approximating the differential equations stemming from the second law,

$$a = \frac{F}{m} = \frac{dv}{dt}$$

and

$$v = \frac{dx}{dt}$$

by the difference equations,

$$a = \frac{v_{new} - v_{old}}{\Delta t}$$

and

$$v = \frac{x_{new} - x_{old}}{\Delta t}$$

Rewriting these equations yields

$$v_{new} = v_{old} + a.\Delta t$$

and

$$x_{new} = x_{old} + v.\Delta t$$

which are now in useful form for application of the so-called Euler method. With this method we effectively 'walk along the curve', calculating and recalculating acceleration (from the present position and a given dependence of force upon position), velocity (from the acceleration), and position (from the new velocity), as the time is incremented again and again by Δt. (Refinements in the technique alter the order of the above steps.)

The simplicity of the technique is clearly evident; the majority of students will follow it with ease. And the power is indeed great. If the force (and therefore the acceleration, through the Second Law) can be expressed as a function of position, as is usually the case, then the method can be applied. And extending the method to velocity dependent forces is technically trivial, requiring only a single-line change in the program.

ICBM I and *II* guide the student toward applying this numerical technique to problem after problem that we pre-computer-age students avoided altogether because of their analytical intractability. The modern student can thus acquire a far richer experience with physical phenomena (albeit simulated) than was previously possible. And the experience with the numerical methods in mechanics lays the basis for using the same methods and their extensions for solving differential equations as they are encountered elsewhere in physics.

The numerical methods by no means replace analytical techniques, but they do dramatically supplement and extend them. Similarly, the CONDUIT packages do not replace traditional textbooks, but they can serve as powerful supplements.

OTHER CONDUIT PACKAGES

PHY057, *Mechanics*, echoes *ICBM I* and *II*, centering on numerical solutions to Newton's Second Law. But unlike these other two packages, Mechanics includes an instructor's guide that provides invaluable discussion of solutions to all the exercises included in the student text.

PHY003, *Using Computers in Physics*, once more repeats the theme of numerically solving the differential equations implicit in the Second Law, but then goes on to apply the numerical methods to a variety of additional topics in physics, ranging from electromagnetic phenomena to quantum mechanics. The general algorithmic approach we have described above, that of having the computer 'walk along a curve' to numerically solve differential equations, recurs in topic after topic in the PHY003 text. Also introduced are algorithms for dealing with statistical physics, techniques for solving simultaneous equations in several unknowns (as for handling electrical circuits), and higher-order Runge-Kutta methods for solving the Schrodinger equation.

Another CONDUIT package by the same author (J. Merrill), PHY006, *Quantum Mechanics*, concentrates exclusively on the title topic, but in a manner similar to PHY003.

The two remaining packages in the present CONDUIT physics series are two CSSP simulations, PHY129, *SCATTER*, and PHY130, *NEWTON*, both similar to *INTERP* in their approach.

THE FUTURE

Several additional packages are under review by CONDUIT and it is likely that some of these and others will be added to the CONDUIT physics series from time to time. But in some ways the more exciting prospects for the future revolve around changes brought about by the widespread availability of the new small stand-alone computer systems, the so-called microcomputers.

The vast numbers of microcomputers coming into use (already hundreds of thousands have been sold in the U.S. alone, as of this writing) have forced CONDUIT to re-examine our past policy of providing only standardized versions of packages. Several of the more popular microcomputers are present in such large numbers that we can now justify the effort of producing and distributing *specialized* versions of our packages for these systems. The benefit to the user is that the specialized versions can now take maximal advantage of the special features of particular systems. Most prominent among these features is a graphical display capability—which all the popular micros support, although the manner of implementation (and the quality) varies from system to system.

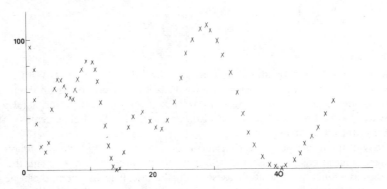

Fig. 8. Example of graphical output for microcomputer version of *INTERP*.

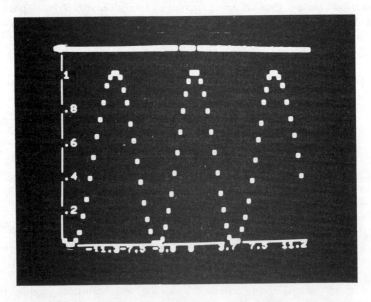

Fig. 9. Example of lower resolution graphical output from a second microcomputer version of
INTERP.

The difference that graphical output can make is dramatic. Figure 8 shows graphical output from PHY183, *INTERP*, approximately as it will appear in one of the specialized microcomputer versions. This should be compared with the tabular output in Fig. 5. Even the much lower resolution of another microcomputer provides acceptable graphical output that is preferable to tables (see Fig. 9).

The contribution of graphics is even more striking, both for its motivational, as well as illustrative value, in the proposed microcomputer versions of *ICBM II*, which will employ displays of the type shown in Fig. 10.

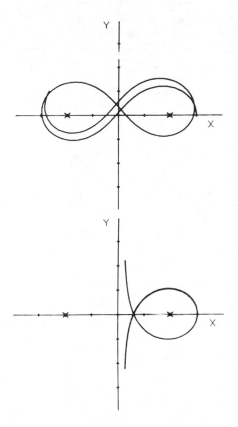

Fig. 10. Samples of graphical output of the type forseen for microcomputer versions of *ICBM II*. (Shown are some sample orbits for motion with two force centers.)

SUMMARY

CONDUIT has reviewed, tested, and now distributes eight packages of computer-based instructional materials in its physics series. Three of the packages are simulations designed primarily to broaden students' experience with certain classes of physical phenomena. The other packages are of the problem-solving type, requiring the student to write programs to solve physics problems, and providing an introduction to numerical methods. But these latter packages also provide much of the physical experience-broadening value of simulations, and in some cases they introduce the student to aspects of computer-based model building as well.

While CONDUIT packages in the past have been distributed only in standardized form, and in the sometimes restrictive languages of FORTRAN and BASIC, specialized versions are now being developed for the new microcomputers, with the distinctive feature of graphical output, and the possibility of some modern languages, such as PASCAL.

CONDUIT's principal objective remains to advance the art of instruction through innovative use of the computer, by identifying quality computer-based materials and making them widely available.

Comput. & Educ., Vol. 4, pp. 11 to 14
Pergamon Press Ltd 1980. Printed in Great Britain

PHYSICS EDUCATION WITH OR WITHOUT COMPUTERS

R. Lewis and J. Harris

Chelsea College, University of London

This paper is the view of a physicist and one time teacher of physics moderated, and hopefully made less idiosyncratic, by another of similar background though, with continued close contact with teaching. I will lean heavily on the experiences of three curriculum development projects using computers with which I have been associated, drawing on the physics content of these whilst reflecting on the views and attitudes of the other sciences.

I was well satisfied with my education as a physicist both at secondary school, at university and during preparation for my research. However, I was no more than an average student, finding difficulty with the huge volume of theory (mathematics) with which I was confronted. Computers played no significant part in this until I came to use software (not fully debugged) to undertake some of the first computerised analysis of seismic wave arrival times. This process was something of a mystery to me but better than string and an electrical calculator despite the tedium of data preparation and frustration of failing Atlas computers. My contact with computers continued intermittently and the fine points of theoretical physics remained something of a mystery. It is only in fairly recent years that I have gained a perspective of theoretical physics as mathematical model building though any competence in this field remains largely dormant.

The purpose of this rather uninteresting tale is to lead into a discussion of what could become the most important role for the computer in physics education. Much of what has been done in the last decade in the use of computers has been to extend the range of a student's investigation of systems as a broadening of their laboratory experiences. In particular I am thinking of simulation of experiments not otherwise possible in a teaching laboratory. (A rather better description of this would be to think of the simulation apparatus as an environment upon which students may perform experiments to help their understanding of the system.) This approach is particularly valuable in allowing students to investigate multi-variate systems where in the real world it is impossible to control many of the variables. Many examples of this kind are found in the life sciences but by and large physics is not quite like that. It is usually possible to take a sample of the 'real-world' into the laboratory, to control the physical variables and expect students to discover something about the system by varying the parameters in a systematic way. Physics laboratories are also well endowed with equipment appropriate for measuring the parameters of physical systems; much of this equipment is cheap, having mass production counterparts in industry. Overall, therefore, the need for simulation in a pseudo-laboratory role in physics is limited. However, there are some examples where this role is valid, for example, units on satellite orbits, and particle scattering (CSSP and CUSC)* since students are unlikely otherwise to have any opportunity to undertake investigations of their own.

One of the objectives of laboratory investigations in physics education is to develop a sense of scientific method. Planning experiments and drawing conclusions from the results are part of this. The objectives for the use of simulation certainly include planning and drawing conclusions about the model used. The latter point is important but basically the value of a simulated investigation is as good and, because of the simplicity of execution, can be better than real experimental work which is often clouded by technical trivia. Let it be emphasised, however, that many of the other objectives of laboratory work can in no sense be achieved through work with computer models.

Closely linked to laboratory type simulations, are those which provide students with the opportunity to 'use' industrial equipment, making the same experimental decisions that are needed in industry or research laboratories. This is especially valuable at secondary level and is exemplified by the units on the Mass Spectrometer and Gas Chromatograph (CC).

However, none of what has been described of simulations would have helped my own understanding of theoretical physics. With the benefit of hindsight and a certain experience of 'doing' physics, it

---

* Examples are quoted at secondary level from the Schools Council Project 'Computers in the Curriculum' (CC), at tertiary level from the Computers in the Undergraduate Science Curriculum (CUSC) Project and at an intermediate level from the Chelsea Science Simulation Project (CSSP) although there are materials from other projects which would serve equally well. Details of these projects may be obtained from Chelsea College in the United Kingdom or from CONDUIT in the United States.

is clear that the large mathematical chunks of my lecture notes were 'asides' in the development of a particular theory. I was often being expected to grapple with unfamiliar mathematical techniques *at the same time* as pursuing aspects of physics which were equally unfamiliar. This is a common failing in teaching—that of introducing more than one new idea at a time.

Is it possible that the computer can help in this area? Any physicist who has been involved in using computers to solve a problem will say that the discipline of writing the program has demanded far more insight into the problem than would be required by a less strict task master. It is often said that one does not fully understand a system unless one has written a computer program to simulate it! If these points are in fact valid then to expect students to write programs to represent theoretical aspects of their study would be to ask a great deal of them.

I believe that the attitude reflected in the previous paragraph—the student writing his own program—reflects computing as it was. The time has now come to view computing in a different light; it must now be looked upon as a way of trying out ideas. To be specific, the availability of interactive graphics provides the *potential* to consider the computer as a laboratory for theoretical ideas; it is becoming possible to 'do' experimental mathematics. At present the language of the computer is not really the language of mathematics. However, this must change in order that the two become not simply isomorphic but identical.

It is necessary to pause a while to consider what is the 'language of mathematics' of our students. It is certainly different from that of experienced theoretical physicists, and will change in the course of their growing awareness. This is, perhaps, the key to the kind of computer language that is needed; it must evolve with the student. At a simple level it must be possible for a student to define a function and have it displayed with a variety of parameter and coefficient values which he has chosen. Students should not have to be concerned with the technicalities of scaling and drawing the graph or of the techniques required to handle, say, the differential equation. The software into which they have simply plugged their relationships and values must allow the students to 'experiment' in the way they may 'experiment' with a simulation of a physical system or with the physical system itself. At a later stage students should be able to supply a series of relationships which they believe represent the behaviour of a real system, that is they should be building models. It is important that the students are fully aware of what they are doing; that they perceive the theoretical aspects of their work as dealing with models. Perhaps it is obvious (but it wasn't to me as a student) that the 'mathematical asides' to which I referred earlier were simply a part of this model building. I think my perception of physics would have been significantly different had I been 'brought up' to think this way.

But to return to the computer language system. As was said earlier it should evolve with the student. In order to achieve this it seems necessary that it has a macro structure which would enable the teacher to define the level of language which should be available to students at a particular time. Thus, at one time the student need not be involved in how their differential equations were being solved, whereas later it may be appropriate for the student to do this. The level of detailed mathematical skill needed to undertake experimental work with the computer should be adjusted to their progress.

In spite of this, it could be argued that, as is possible with statistics, students would gain only a superficial or cookbook knowledge of important areas of mathematics. This is indeed a danger but it is one over which the teacher has control; the teacher has much less control over the confused minds of students who are taught in more traditional ways.

Without going quite so far along the road of student model-building, it is possible to design CAL material in which students choose between a series of models or have the opportunity to make simple changes to existing models (INTERP and NEWTON in CSSP). As is possible in INTERP this kind of investigation is best linked to real laboratory work so providing the student with the full range of experimentation, analysis and interpretation confronting the physicist.

So far we have been concerned with the computer as a resource for students' learning. Physics students, in common with students of other sciences and in fact with students of all disciplines, should be aware of the role of computers in physics and have at least some skill in putting them to use. In all of the learning processes students will become involved in using computers to do something useful *for them*. This is an extremely good introduction to their own study of certain aspects of physics and they should go on to be taught the principles of information processing and a working knowledge of a widely used programming language. One other aspect of computer use which will certainly become commonplace in their lifetimes in whatever branch of physics they become involved, is the real-time handling of data from experiments. The use of laboratory mini-computers for data capture, analysis and experimental control is already quite common; the ubiquitous 'chip' will find its way into practically every field during the next decade. To give students relevant experience demands that we design specific experiments illustrating the use of micro-processors and involve students in as much (or as little) of the nuts and bolts of interfacing, timing, data conditioning etc. as it is felt appropriate for his particular course. This kind of activity should certainly begin at secondary or high school.

I seem to have come round full circle to aspects of laboratory work which will doubtless be different in the near future. However, it does seem that the greatest potential for advances in physics education lies in the field of experimental theoretical work with the computer; this may not (should not) replace work with paper and pencil but will act as a necessary new dimension.

Having been through a kaleidoscope of 'things physicists do', it may be useful to go back and provide rather more detailed information on CAL in physics teaching in Britain which is less speculative. This may be familiar to those who have been able to keep informed about developments here. As earlier, this is necessarily biased in the emphasis it gives to those projects in which we have been involved.

Between 1972 and 1975 Chelsea College supported the Chelsea Science Simulation Project. The intention was to explore the contribution that computer simulations could make to the teaching of science in secondary schools, largely in the 16–19 year old range. Because of earlier specialisation in British schools the material produced may be useful for introductory University or College courses in the United States. Ten packages were produced in biology, chemistry and physics[1]. Each package consists of Students' Notes, Teachers' Guide, program in BASIC and program documentation and are obtainable in the United States through CONDUIT[2]. The three physics packages deal with: Satellite orbits (NEWTON), particle scattering (SCATTER), and superposition of waves (INTERP). While these are favourite topics for computer simulations, the approach taken, which attempts to emphasise to students the role of a model in understanding physical phenomena, may be of interest. For example, in SCATTER students are led to think about the different scattering patterns predicted by a 'hard sphere' model for the nucleus, as well as the inverse-square force law. Later, when presented with some simulated experimental results for scattering of alpha-particles by a metal foil they are asked to decide which model was used in the computer program that produced the results. They should be able to do this on the basis of the predictions made by the two models, and how the scattering pattern varies with various experimental factors (particle energy, thickness of foil and so on). The interactive computer program allows them to plan and carry out an investigation to find out which model was used in the program.

Starting in 1973 the Schools Council—a publicly financed body with responsibility for curriculum and examinations in schools—sponsored the Computers in the Curriculum Project. So far material in biology, chemistry, physics, economics and geography has been published[3]. Phase Two of the project has been funded and will end in 1981.

The physics packages in this series deal with: photoelectric effect, mass spectrometer, gravitational fields, planetary motion, capacitor discharge, radio-active decay and gaseous diffusion. The emphasis is often on the simulation of a piece of apparatus not available in a school laboratory. All the programs are designed for interactive use, and the audience is again 16–19 year olds who are specialising in physics and two or three other subjects.

A notable exception is HOME HEATING[4], which is aimed at the 13–16 year range. A common practical activity is to measure the effectiveness of various materials as heat insulators[5], and this might be followed by a discussion of the fuel savings that would ensue from more efficient insulation of our homes.

The computer program allows students to explore this quantitatively. The relevant factors (size, location, building material, area of windows, and so on) are input. (To allow for the student who does not know all the relevant details of his home, 'default values', typical of the average home, are used for parameters which the student does not specify.) The program calculates the annual cost of heating the house, with various fuels at current prices, and the savings possible by installing double glazing, roof insulation and so on can be investigated.

The programs described so far were all developed for use in schools which had access to a computer through a printing or visual display terminal. The rapid advent of micro-computers, with the possibility of graphical displays will allow the presentation of many of them to be improved. These technological advances, are being capitalised on in the second phase of the Computers in the Curriculum project as high resolution graphics allows the presentation of more elucide descriptions of systems and models.

It is impossible in a short review to mention all the work in the different physics departments in British Universities. CUSC (Computers in the Undergraduate Science Curriculum) was one of the projects of the National Development Programme in Computer Assisted Learning (NDPCAL)—a £2 million project which ran from 1973 to 1977[6]. When describing the physics materials[7] McKenzie says:

"In general, the computer is used by setting up a simulation, or mathematical model, of the physical system under study; the student can then explore the system by changing various parameters and thinking about their effect on the system as demonstrated by the graphical presentation. Use of graphics *per se* would hardly be novel, since the use of pictures in print, slide or film stretches back over decades; the extra feature is the use of 'interaction', whereby the terminal not only offers the possibility of touching a key to change the display, but also requires it. A student must remain sufficiently alert to take some action, otherwise the display will continue unchanged. The action taken may vary widely, from the simplest example of repeatedly touching a key, to the more elaborate case of deciding on a strategy and changing parameters accordingly, but in one way or another he must keep his wits about him and be an active participant. Contrast this to hearing a lecture!"

The physics programs of CUSC—all of which use graphics—include the Schrodinger Potential Well and Barrier, Phasors and Multiphasors, Satellite Motion, Rutherford Scattering, Fourier Series and Moments of Inertia.

Other developments under the NDPCAL umbrella which might be of interest to physics teachers— though they actually took place in Engineering Departments—are in the fluid mechanics laboratory at Imperial College, and the Nuclear Engineering Department at Queen Mary College[8].

The Computational Physics Teaching Laboratory supported by NDPCAL at Surrey University[9] has developed some packages of material but the emphasis has been on students developing their own alphanumeric programs (in BASIC) based on problem solving and model building examples arising from tutorial and lecture classes. At Cambridge in the Department of Applied Mathematics and Theoretical Physics more advanced problem solving has been undertaken by students in projects using graphics to display the predictions of their models[10]. This work pre-dates NDPCAL and was developed despite the limited language facilities then available. It is anticipated that substantial advances will be made as new computing facilities come into use during 1979.

And so again we return to the place where computers first made their contribution to our under- standing of physics—to models and problem solving—but not now the domain of the advanced researcher only, but of our students in schools and colleges. The signs are that this involvement can contribute to skills beyond those directly inculcated and the exciting thing is that we are only just beginning to realise the computer's potential.

REFERENCES

1. *Chelsea Science Simulation Project* (packs of Students and Teachers material). Edward Arnold, London (1975–7).
2. CONDUIT, P.O. Box 388, Iowa City, IA 52240.
3. *Computers in the Physics Curriculum.* Schools Council/Edward Arnold, London (1978); *Computers in the Biology Curriculum.* Schools Council/Edward Arnold, London (1978); *Computers in the Economics Curricu- lum.* Schools Council/Edward Arnold, London (1978); *Computers in the Chemistry Curriculum.* Schools Council/Edward Arnold, London (1979); *Computers in the Geography Curriculum.* Schools Council/Edward Arnold, London (1979).
4. *Computers in the Curriculum—Home Heating.* Schools Council/Edward Arnold, London (1979).
5. For example: *Science for the 70's* (Edited by Mee, Boyd and Ritchie) 2nd edn, Book 2, p. 9. Heineman, London (1974); or *Insight to Science, Air and Heat* (Edited by Inner London Education Authority) Addison- Wesley, London (1978).
6. *NDPCAL, Final Report.* Council for Educational Technology, London (1977).
7. *Interactive Computer Graphics in Science Teaching* (Edited by McKenzie, Elton and Lewis) Ellis Horwood, Chichester (1978) (materials from Educational Computing Section, Chelsea College, Pulton Place, London SW6 5PR).
8. *Engineering Sciences Project.* Faculty of Engineering, Queen Mary College, Mile End Road, London E1 4NS.
9. *Computational Physics Teaching Laboratory.* Department of Physics, University of Surrey, Guildford, Surrey.
10. *DAMTP.* Cambridge University, Silver Street, Cambridge, CB3 9EW.

Comput. & Educ., Vol. 4, pp. 15 to 36
Pergamon Press Ltd 1980. Printed in Great Britain

A COMPUTER-BASED COURSE IN CLASSICAL MECHANICS

D. KANE and B. SHERWOOD

Department of Physics,
University of Illinois at Urbana-Champaign

HISTORY

Starting in 1970, some computer-based lessons dealing with classical mechanics were created on the PLATO III system, and by 1971 enough topics had been covered to permit offering some lessons to an experimental section of ten students. The initial stimulus was a recognition that many topics, such as free-body diagrams, involved so many details as to be very difficult to teach in lectures or small-group discussion classes. Every year, students brought the same kinds of confusion to instructor office hours, where a great deal of individual attention was needed to bring the student to the point of being able to integrate the many concepts involved in solving mechanics problems. It was hoped that individualized computer-based instruction could provide a floor of basic understanding which would help students directly and also make possible enriched lectures and class discussions based on this understanding.

As the PLATO IV system [1] began to develop, ten new terminals were placed temporarily in the Department for testing purposes, and existing physics lessons were converted to the new system. A National Science Foundation contract provided thirty terminals on a permanent basis to the Department of Physics, and these terminals were placed in a single room to make it possible to handle scheduled classes (most of our introductory physics courses are divided into sections of 20–25 students). In addition to providing a remodeled room for the terminals, the Department of Physics facilitated curriculum development by partially funding some senior staff, by hiring a full-time PLATO staff member for the department, and by assigning graduate-student teaching assistants to PLATO-related activities. The Department at a very early stage included PLATO activities in its long-range planning and budgeting within the University.

The availability of the physics PLATO classroom made it possible not only to develop and test individual lessons but also to gain experience in integrating these materials with regularly scheduled classes on a large scale. It was decided to write computer-based materials to accompany the standard calculus-based mechanics course for engineering and science freshmen [2]. It was tempting to create an entirely new and different course, perhaps self-placed, but it was felt that the computer-based medium was so novel in itself that it would be unwise to make drastic changes in course content and organization at the same time that a new medium was being explored.

Additional lessons were written in parallel with the continued development of the PLATO IV system, and by 1975 sizable numbers of students were enrolled in the PLATO-based version of the course. At present (1979) the physics PLATO classroom is nearly saturated with 500 students, each of whom use about 4 h per week of terminal time during a 16-week semester. (Some of this study is done at other PLATO sites on the campus.) Figure 1 shows the physics PLATO classroom. This facility is also used for scheduled activities in some other courses from time to time during a given semester. Various calculational features of PLATO are also used on an informal basis by faculty members and graduate students.

In addition to the classical mechanics materials described here, computer-based materials have also been written for sophomore-level physics (optics, waves, and introductory quantum mechanics) and for upper-level and graduate courses in nuclear physics and quantum mechanics [3].

SAMPLE LESSONS

Several different kinds of lessons are used in this course. The most important categories are tutorial lessons and homework exercises. The tutorial lessons attempt to tutor the student in the fundamental concepts associated with a topic, starting from nothing and leading to simple applications. The homework exercises provide on-line checking of student answers to problems which are similar to the more difficult problems found in typical textbooks, with extensive help sequences available. In addition to these two major categories there are many other kinds of materials available, including drills

Fig. 1. The Department of Physics of the University of Illinois (Urbana-Champaign) has a
32-terminal PLATO classroom.

of various sorts, physics-oriented games, review problems[4], calculational and plotting routines, and
an on-line gradebook. The students can also write electronic notes to their instructors and can discuss
questions of interest to students and instructors in an on-line forum.

An example of a tutorial lesson is one dealing with two-dimensional kinematics[5]. Figure 2 shows
the title page, statement of purpose, and table of contents from this lesson. Note that the statement of
purpose also specifies prerequisites. In our use of the lesson, students normally must complete lessons

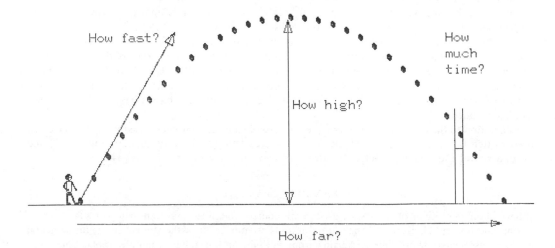

PURPOSE

The purpose of this lesson is to illustrate motion

in two dimensions. The examples deal with gravita-

tional motion. We will kick a football, both

on a football field (constant acceleration) and

around a planetoid (circular motion at constant

speed).

It is assumed that you have been introduced to

vector notation. It is also assumed that you have

studied one-dimensional motion at constant

acceleration.

Table of Contents for "Two-dimensional Kinematics"

You can press BACK to return to where you were.
   Choose a topic: ⟩

```
+-----------------------------------------------+
| You can return to this index page at          |
| any time by pressing shift-DATA.              |
+-----------------------------------------------+
```

Fig. 2. Title page, statement of purpose, and table of contents for a lesson on two-dimensional kinematics. Notice the asterisks on the table of contents, which remind the student which sections he or she has completed.

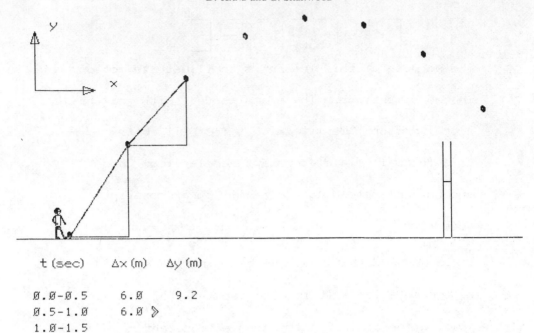

t (sec)	Δx (m)	Δy (m)
0.0-0.5	6.0	9.2
0.5-1.0	6.0	≫
1.0-1.5		
1.5-2.0		
2.0-2.5		
2.5-3.0		

Measure Δy, the vertical displacement.

Fig. 3(a).

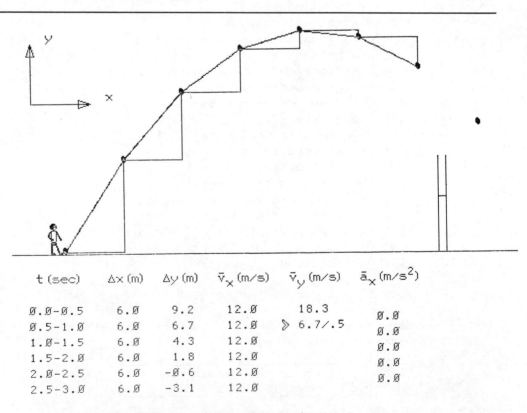

t (sec)	Δx (m)	Δy (m)	$\bar{v}_x$ (m/s)	$\bar{v}_y$ (m/s)	$\bar{a}_x$ (m/s^2)
0.0-0.5	6.0	9.2	12.0	18.3	0.0
0.5-1.0	6.0	6.7	12.0	≫ 6.7/.5	0.0
1.0-1.5	6.0	4.3	12.0		0.0
1.5-2.0	6.0	1.8	12.0		0.0
2.0-2.5	6.0	-0.6	12.0		0.0
2.5-3.0	6.0	-3.1	12.0		

Calculate $\bar{v}_y = \Delta y / \Delta t$, where $\Delta t = 0.5$ sec.

Fig. 3(b).

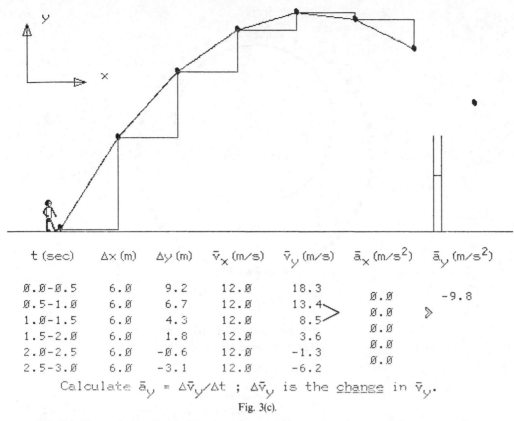

t (sec)	Δx (m)	Δy (m)	$\bar{v}_x$ (m/s)	$\bar{v}_y$ (m/s)	$\bar{a}_x$ (m/s^2)	$\bar{a}_y$ (m/s^2)
0.0-0.5	6.0	9.2	12.0	18.3		-9.8
0.5-1.0	6.0	6.7	12.0	13.4	0.0	
1.0-1.5	6.0	4.3	12.0	8.5	0.0	
1.5-2.0	6.0	1.8	12.0	3.6	0.0	
2.0-2.5	6.0	-0.6	12.0	-1.3	0.0	
2.5-3.0	6.0	-3.1	12.0	-6.2	0.0	

Calculate $\bar{a}_y = \Delta\bar{v}_y/\Delta t$; $\Delta\bar{v}_y$ is the change in $\bar{v}_y$.

Fig. 3(c).

Fig. 3(a). The student makes screen measurements with a paper ruler prepared on a preceding page. (b) The student calculates average velocity components from the data. (c) The student calculates the average acceleration.

on these prerequisites before studying this lesson, but this is a function of the 'routing' to be discussed later, not a function of the lesson itself, which in principle can be used by other teachers in a different way than we use it. As can be seen from the table of contents, the introduction of new concepts and terminology alternates with check-up sets of questions on the new material. Note that the student can press a single key at any time to return to the table of contents. This makes it easy for the student to skip over known material or to review earlier material. The asterisks shown beside the table of contents remind the student which sections have already been completed, even if that work was done weeks before.

Many different techniques are used to illustrate concepts. Graphics are used heavily, as is shown in the sequence of Fig. 3, which shows how the student is asked to measure distances on the screen (this is followed by analysis of the acquired data). Figure 4 shows how circular motion is introduced in terms of Newton's argument about throwing an object around the world from a high mountain. Here the student is invited to explore what happens when a football is kicked on a small planetoid. This simulation leads into having the student work through a proof that radial acceleration is v^2/r, with the student carrying out many of the steps. In the course of the proof the student types algebraic expressions whose correctness is checked by simple techniques available in the TUTOR language[6] in which PLATO lessons are written. The simulation and proof are followed by applications to satellite motion.

The check-up questions interspersed throughout the lesson consist of simple problems whose parameters are chosen randomly, and which appear in random order. If the student gets a question wrong, or if the student has to ask for help, the question reappears later in the drill (with different random parameters). The presentation of each problem at least once is facilitated by TUTOR commands for manipulating a permutation sequence of numbers. A typical question is shown in Fig. 5.

The last section of the lesson is a 'mastery quiz' in which the student must answer six out of eight questions correctly to get credit for finishing the lesson. The questions are drawn from the check-up questions and other interactions within the lesson, but with the difference that no help is provided and the answers must be correct on the first try (simple errors such as unbalanced parentheses are not counted as tries). The student can choose to take the final quiz at any time, even without studying the

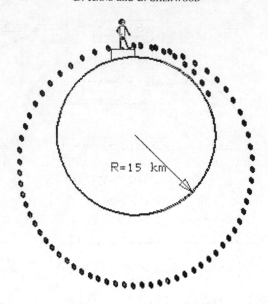

You are standing on a small planetoid.
Pick a kicking speed and see what happens!

≫   m/s

Press BACK to clean up screen, shift-BACK to quit.

Fig. 4. Animated simulation of Newton's argument concerning gravitational motion around the earth. The student has tried two different initial speeds.

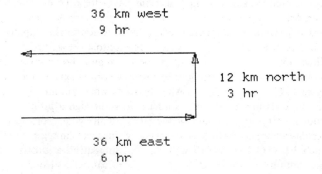

A hiker walks east, then north, then west, taking varying amounts of time, as shown.

What is the magnitude of the average velocity?

v̄ = ≫ 12km/18hr

Fig. 5. An example of a quiz problem. The numerical factors are chosen randomly.

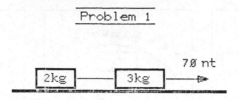

```
                    Problem 1
```

```
                                            7Ø nt
              ┌────┐        ┌────┐
              │2kg │────────│3kg │────▷
              └────┘        └────┘
```

```
    A 3 kg block and a 2 kg block are tied together and
    are pulled across the floor by a force of 7Ø newtons.
    The coefficient of friction of the blocks with the
    floor is   µ = Ø.5 .


    What is the acceleration of the two blocks?


        ▷
```

```
  Press SHIFT-LAB to use the calculator;   Press BACK to return
```

Fig. 6. An example of the kind of problem found in the on-line problem sets.

tutorial material. The quiz can be repeated as many times as the student wishes, but the questions appear in different orders with different numbers and other parameters.

The other major category of materials is illustrated by a set of on-line homework problems dealing with dynamics [7]. Figure 6 shows one of the eight problems in this set, which deals with blocks, strings, pulleys, and circular motion. Students are given printed copies of these problems, but with standard parameters different from those generated on-line for each student, on the basis of the student's name. The students are encouraged to work out the problems algebraically at home, then answer their particular numerical problems at a terminal, though many students work directly at a terminal. Responses which have bad form (unbalanced parentheses, square roots of negative numbers, etc.) yield appropriate comments on the error. If no units are given, the student is asked to give the units. If incorrect units are given, the student is told 'Those aren't units of acceleration!' (or whatever the quantity is). If the response has proper form and correct units but is incorrect, the student is told that it is wrong, and that help is available. The correct answer is not given, which makes this checking somewhat different from looking at answers in the back of a textbook, where the display of the correct answer often encourages the student to twist the solution to obtain that particular answer. There are 14 problem sets of this type, covering all major topics of a classical mechanics course, with four alternative sets for use with textbooks which treat energy before momentum rather than momentum before energy. The problems in these sets are rather difficult. In particular, they are typically quite a bit more difficult than the simple applications and quiz problems appearing in the tutorial lessons. There have been complaints that there is therefore often a gap between the level of difficulty of the tutorial and of the homework problems associated with that tutorial, and that the tutorial lesson should go further in illustrating applications.

If the student asks for help (by pressing the 'help' key), a full discussion of the problem is given. In the problem set dealing with dynamics, this help takes the form of a rapid review of the methodology of how to solve dynamics problems by systematic analysis, a topic covered in earlier tutorial lessons. Figure 7 shows major points in the help sequence. Touch input is used to speed up and simplify the interaction: even the algebraic equations are entered merely by touching appropriate terms on the screen. Forces are identified in terms of the source objects ('earth' instead of 'gravity', 'table' instead of 'friction', and 'string' instead of 'tension'). This procedure emphasizes that neighboring objects are the

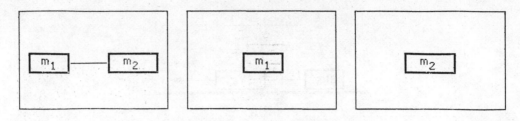

Pick a system by pointing at the one you want.

Touch the name of an object that exerts a force on your system.

person
pulling   floor   string   earth m_1 m_2

TOUCH HERE when
you think you
have found all
the forces.

Touch the name of an object that exerts a force on your system.

person
pulling   floor   string   earth m_1 m_2

TOUCH HERE when
you think you
have found all
the forces.

Fig. 7.

Write the x-component of the eqn. of motion (by touch):

F   g N_1 N_2 μ   T

m_1 a_{1x} a_{1y}

+   −   (   )   ∅   =

ERASE   ERASE   HELP   DONE
               ALL

Write the x-component of the eqn. of motion (by touch):

$m_1 a_{1x}$ =

F   g N_1 N_2 μ   T

m_1 a_{1x} a_{1y}

+   −   (   )   ∅   =

ERASE   ERASE   HELP   DONE
               ALL

Fig. 7.

Write the x-component of the eqn. of motion (by touch):

$m_1 a_{1x} = T - \mu N_1$ ok

Write the y-component of the eq. of motion:

F	g	N_1	N_2	μ	T

m_1 a_{1x} a_{1y}

+   −   (   )   Ø   =

ERASE   ERASE
                ALL   HELP   DONE

Write the x-component of the eqn. of motion (by touch):

$m_1 a_{1x} = T - \mu N_1$ ok

Write the y-component of the eq. of motion:

$N_1 - m_1 g = m_1 a_{1y}$ ok

F	g	N_1	N_2	μ	T

Copy these equations into your notebook, then press NEXT.

m_1 a_{1x} a_{1y}

+   −   (   )   Ø   =

ERASE   ERASE
                ALL   HELP   DONE

Fig. 7.

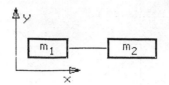

If the string doesn't stretch or
slacken, the blocks are "constrained"
to accelerate together at some rate
"a". Also, the floor constrains the
blocks to move horizontally.

Complete the geometrical constraint equations (by touch):

a_{1x} = → a_{2x} =

a_{1y} = a_{2y} =

---

      a

("a" is the unknown acceleration of the right block)

     +   -   (   )   Ø   /

     ERASE   ERASE   HELP   DONE
                    ALL

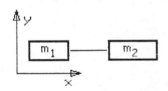

If the string doesn't stretch or
slacken, the blocks are "constrained"
to accelerate together at some rate
"a". Also, the floor constrains the
blocks to move horizontally.

Complete the geometrical constraint equations (by touch):

a_{1x} =   a   ok a_{2x} =   a   ok

a_{1y} =   Ø   ok a_{2y} =   Ø   ok

Write these constraints in your notebook, then press NEXT.

---

      a

("a" is the unknown acceleration of the right block)

     +   -   (   )   Ø   /

     ERASE   ERASE   HELP   DONE
                    ALL

Fig. 7.

Here are the equations of motion and of constraint:

$$m_1 a = T - \mu N_1$$

$$\emptyset = N_1 - m_1 g$$

$$m_2 a = F - T - \mu N_2$$

$$\emptyset = N_2 - m_2 g$$

$$a_{1x} = a$$

$$a_{1y} = \emptyset$$

SUBSTITUTE

$$a_{2x} = a$$

$$a_{2y} = \emptyset$$

As the first step in solving these equations, it helps to simplify them by substituting the constraints into the equations of motion.

Here are the equations of motion and of constraint:

$$m_1 a_{1x} = T - \mu N_1$$

$$m_1 a_{1y} = N_1 - m_1 g$$

$$m_2 a_{2x} = F - T - \mu N_2$$

$$m_2 a_{2y} = N_2 - m_2 g$$

$$a_{1x} = a$$

$$a_{1y} = \emptyset$$

SUBSTITUTE

$$a_{2x} = a$$

$$a_{2y} = \emptyset$$

As the first step in solving these equations, it helps to simplify them by substituting the constraints into the equations of motion.

Fig. 7. Major steps in the help sequence accompanying the problem shown in Fig. 6. The use of touch input speeds up and simplifies the interaction.

sources of forces, and prevents the introduction of pseudo-forces such as the 'centrifugal force'. Geometrical constraints are kept separate from dynamical equations. The help sequence ends up showing the student how to manipulate the equations to reduce them to a manageable set.

The question of how much and what kind of help to provide is a perplexing one. Originally we provided no help other than pointing out format and units errors to the student. It quickly became clear that students were not ready to approach such problems on their own with only the preparation of the tutorial lessons. Discussion class meetings and individual tutoring sessions were being devoted to repetition of the solution of the PLATO problem sets. It seemed that PLATO could be providing these standard discussions, thus allowing the instructor to address more individualized needs in face-to-face meetings with the students. This, along with the difficulty of the problems, and the impossibility of diagnosing by program what conceptual or calculational error had been made (except for some common mistakes), eventually forced us to offer full help sequences for all the problems. This does make it possible for a student simply to stumble through the (interactive) discussion to find the answer, with little understanding or effort. Most students realize that they must use the help

```
    Design Curriculum Modules          "ph106x0"
    15 in use        20 maximum         "phys106i"


    NAME/(TYPE)      # ITEMS       CRITERIA


  1   intro            2      Complete 2 lessons OR
      (index)                 Move ahead on 1/29/79 (force)
                              Next:  2 Back: (none)


  2   vectors          4      Score 1 on lesson 5 OR
      (index)                 Move ahead on 1/29/79 (force)
                              Next:  3 Back: 1


  3   1d-kin           4      Score 90 on lesson 8 OR
      (index)                 Move ahead on 1/29/79 (force)
                              Next:  4 Back: 2


  4   2d-kin           4      Score 90 on lesson 10 OR
      (index)                 Move ahead on 2/5/79 (force)
                              Next:  5 Back: 3


  5   choose           1      Complete lesson 75 (force)
      (index)                 Next:  6 Back: 4



    See/Revise Module Number:  >      (or NEXT for more)
       HELP available
       DATA to start a new module
       LAB  to change module progression
  shift-LAB  to change module titles
```

Fig. 10. Partial listing of modules of instruction, showing the criteria specified by the instructor
for passing from one module to another.

influenced not only the form and content of the materials but also suggested how such materials might best be integrated into the course structure. In order to explain the organizational structure arrived at, it is useful to sketch the structure of the traditional form of the course in this department.

The standard course has two 1-h lectures per week in a large lecture hall holding several hundred students. These lectures present basic theory, methods for treating various applications of the theory, and live demonstrations of physical phenomena. The students also meet in small groups (20–25 students) twice a week in 2-h sessions with an instructor who is either a senior faculty member or a graduate-student teaching assistant. One of these 2-h periods is a discussion session centered on how to work the assigned homework problems, and a short quiz is often given. The other weekly session is either a lab experiment (five or six in a 16-week semester) or an additional discussion session. Readings and homework problems are assigned from a standard textbook, but normally homework is not collected. There are three 1-h exams during the semester and a 3-h final exam.

After several iterations, the PLATO version of the course has ended up with the following organization. There is only one lecture per week instead of two, thanks to the detailed presentations provided by the computer-based materials. Also, the remaining lecture places somewhat less emphasis on teaching theory and solutions and more emphasis on demonstrations, scientific context, etc. The discussion period has been changed into a scheduled workshop in the PLATO classroom, with the instructor present to answer questions that arise as students study on their own. It is feasible for the instructor to give a good deal of individual assistance, since the bulk of the time the students are intently studying at the terminals. The other two-hour meeting each week is a standard discussion period and does not involve PLATO. The instructor answers questions, works through problems of general interest and gives quizzes during this period or conducts a laboratory exercise if one is scheduled that week. Instructors receive up-to-date information on what PLATO materials have been

sequences sparingly if they are to really learn the material. Some students, however, do seem to have trouble remembering that the main object of the exercise is to learn the material and not just to get the computer to accept an answer and let them go on. It does seem necessary at some point to present problems with no help available if only to keep students honest with themselves about how much they really know on their own. Since help has been added to the PLATO problem sets, this aspect of the course has been handled by off-line quizzes and, of course, by the periodic exams. (The quizzes at the end of lessons offer no help, but these quizzes involve simpler questions than those of the homework problems.) It seems natural eventually to make some kind of such self-testing available once again on PLATO.

The recommended study sequence is the tutorial lesson followed by the homework problems. In principle a student could try the homework problems first, asking for help where necessary, and back into the tutorial as a review of the theory behind the applications. Most students do however study the tutorial lessons before attempting the homework problems.

The stress on the notion of a subsystem with the associated emphasis on free-body diagrams, as illustrated in the help sequence just described, is perhaps the only major innovation in the *content* of the course (as opposed to the unusual nature of the computer-based medium itself). Another example[8] of this may be seen in Fig. 8, where the student must compose (by touching the various terms) the work-energy equation for a system made up of the earth, a dumbbell, and the woman who lifts the dumbbell. The student must also write work-energy equations in a similar way for other choices of system (dumbbell alone, dumbbell plus woman, and dumbbell plus earth). The point of the exercise is to show how the form of the work-energy equation changes for different choices of system. In particular, individual terms shift from one side of the equation to the other depending on whether the associated object is included or excluded from the system. This lesson also discusses the distinction between the true dynamical work-energy equation and the essentially kinematical pseudo-work-energy equation obtained by integrating the equation of motion for the center-of-mass point ($\Sigma F = Ma_{cm}$)[9].

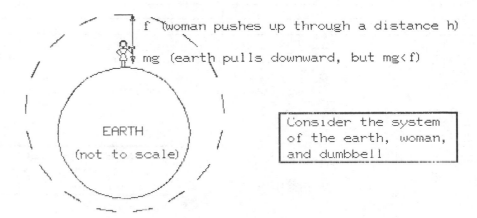

```
   f (woman pushes up through a distance h)
   mg (earth pulls downward, but mg<f)

   EARTH              Consider the system
   (not to scale)     of the earth, woman,
                      and dumbbell
```

How much WORK is done on the system? (Touch the boxes, and touch DONE to have your expression checked.)

W   =

4 problems to go

fh	mgh	$mv_f^2/2$	$mv_i^2/2$	ΔU_{woman}

+	−	0	ERASE	DONE

Fig. 8.

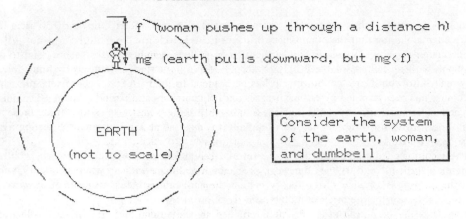

Now write the change in energy of the system.

$$W \quad = \quad \Delta E$$

$$0 \ =$$

4 problems to go

fh	mgh	$mv_f^2/2$	$mv_i^2/2$	ΔU_{woman}

+	−	0	ERASE	DONE

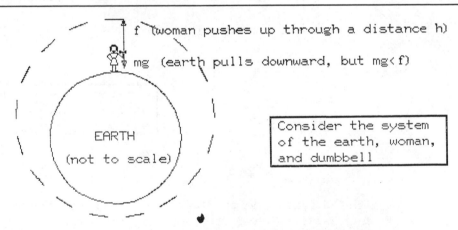

Now write the change in energy of the system.

$$W \quad = \quad \Delta E$$

$$0 \ = \ mv_f^2/2 \ - \ mv_i^2/2 \ + \ mgh \ + \ \Delta U_{woman} \qquad \text{(ok)}$$

3 problems to go

fh	mgh	$mv_f^2/2$	$mv_i^2/2$	ΔU_{woman}

+	−	0	ERASE	DONE

Fig. 8. The student constructs (by touch) the work-energy equation for various choices of system (here the system is the universe, consisting of earth, woman, and dumbbell).

ROUTING

Students are routed among the available materials by a standard PLATO facility, the 'module router'. A router is a program which can be specified to handle students as they sign into the system. A router typically offers the student a choice of lessons to study, keeps track in a database of the progress of the student, and holds enough status to permit the student to go back into a lesson to resume studying where the student had left off, possibly days or weeks before. The module router is a router particularly well suited to managing university courses. It makes it easy for instructors to set up 'modules' of instruction consisting of sets of lessons for a particular topic, to specify simple criteria for moving from one module to another, and to receive summaries of student progress in terms of lessons 'completed' (typically a lesson returns completion information to the router based on performance in a mastery quiz) and numerical scores (the homework sets hand the router a numerical score for the problems done).

Figure 9 shows a typical module page offered to the student upon signing into the system. Figure 10 shows a partial listing of the modules which make up the classical mechanics course, with criteria for proceeding from one module to the next.

COURSE ORGANIZATION

One of the most important problems we have wrestled with is how best to integrate the computer-based materials with other components of the course (lecture, discussion sections, lab, textbook, and exams). We have already discussed some of the reasons for writing computer-based materials, which

```
Rotational Dynamics    (page 1 of 2)

   REQUIRED LESSONS:
   a    Overview of rotational dynamics  (r)
   b    Torque and angular momentum  (r)

   To receive full credit for "a" and "b", you
   must complete them no later than Sun Apr 8.

   Optional activities:
   c    Moment of inertia and rotational kinetic energy
   d    Radian measure (may be review for you)
   e    Right hand rule: drill and practice
   f    Torque games: light/middle/heavy-wts

   REQUIRED LESSONS:
   g    Problem set 10: rotational dynamics  (r)
   h    Free-body diagrams with rotation  (r)

   To receive full credit for "g" and "h", you
   must complete them no later than Sun Apr 15.

   i    Miscellaneous aids
```

Choose a letter, or press one of these keys:
   SHIFT-STOP to sign off
   BACK for previous lessons   NEXT for more lessons
   HELP for explanation

Fig. 9. A typical module of instruction. The student merely chooses a letter to study the chosen lesson.

Scores and lessons completed for group ph106x1:

05/21/79

	Overview of ranges and range of...	Torque and measure	Median and insure	Right question rule	Torque problem games:	Problem embodiment set:1	Free-body diagram:10:	Miscellaneous...		Tot.	Av.
barber	*	*	*			+	100	*	+	100	100
bendel	*	*					36	-	+	36	36
boyle	*	*	*	*	+	+	100	*	+	100	100
ericson	*	*	-	-		+	100	*	+	100	100
fagan	*	-							+		
gibson	*	*	*		-	+	100	*	+	100	100
giles	*	*		*		+	29	-	+	29	29
gonzales	*	*	-	-	+	+	100	*	+	100	100
heath	*	*	*	*	+		91		+	91	91
holloway	*	*	*	*	+	+	100	*	+	100	100
hughes	*	*	*	-	+	+	91		+	91	91
jones	*	*	*	-			100	*	+	100	100
keene	*	*	-	*			100	*	+	100	100
mckay	*	*	*			+	100	*	+	100	100
nathan	*	*	*	*	+	+	100	*	+	100	100
pope	*	*	*	*	-		100	*	+	100	100
porter	*	*	-		+	+	100	*	+	100	100
shields	*	*	-				100	*	+	100	100
strong	*				+	+	0		+	0	0

(*) completed lessons; (-) incomplete lessons;
(+) lessons with no real "end"

Fig. 11. An example of the kind of report used by instructors to catch problems and to plan class discussions.

completed by their students. This provides a detailed basis for planning what aspects to emphasize in this class discussion. The timeliness of this information, and its much greater detail, make it easier for instructors to spot students who are falling behind and who need special attention. Figure 11 shows an example of the kinds of reports instructors use for planning and tracking purposes. The PLATO lessons have been written in such a way as to be usable with a wide range of standard textbooks, and several different textbooks have in fact been used in the course. The role of the textbook is somewhat less important than in the non-PLATO version of the course, since the computer-based lessons typically cover the material in greater detail. However, the textbook serves an important purpose as a portable reference source. Exams are the same in the two versions of the course.

It was mentioned that students are observed to spend about 4 h per week at a terminal, 2 h of which is the scheduled time with their instructor and 1 h can be counted as the missing lecture, leaving 1 h of other self-scheduled terminal use. Instructors are on duty in the PLATO classroom at popular times to answer questions.

The completion of the more important PLATO materials (tutorials on major topics, and the associated homework sets, but not certain optional materials) counts toward the course grade. Typically this has been 25% of the grade, with 30% for the final exam, 30% for the three 1-h exams, and 15% for lab work. In a certain sense, counting the PLATO work in the grade substitutes for grading homework or in-class short quizzes. No significant attempt is made to insure that the PLATO work is actually the student's own work, and there seems to be no real problem with this. In fact, we encourage students at adjacent terminals to help each other, because we feel that their conversations will assist them in understanding the concepts.

Because we want students to complete PLATO materials before attending the related class discussion, and in order to keep the students on schedule in preparing for the periodic exams, we experimented with various incentives for turning in work on time. We experimented for several semesters with allowing access to various computer games for students who were up to date with their course work. This was very popular with many students but eventually was dropped for a number of reasons. It made the management of the PLATO classroom quite difficult and time-consuming, since at any given time some of the students in the room were trying to study while others were playing and talking. It also cast the computer-based physics materials in a curious role. The lessons became for some students primarily a barrier to be overcome on the way to the games. Also, as the numbers of students in the computer-based version of the course increased, the amount of time available for such experimental recreational use decreased. We also tried a scheme under which no credit was given for a lesson completed after a given date. We found, however, that with such a severe penalty, some students were rushing through the material as quickly as possible just to get it done. We have settled on a system under which we give full credit for a lesson if it is completed by a certain date and about 10% less if it is completed later. This has proven to be quite satisfactory in motivating most students to keep caught up. Through the on-line gradebook, they are able to see a distribution of everyone's cumulative score on the PLATO work on a day-to-day basis, and since this score counts about 20% in their overall course grade, there is a natural tendency to not want to fall behind.

Because almost all physics departments have involved students in using the computer as a computer, to calculate and to simulate, we felt there was no need for us to duplicate this work and concentrated rather on the less common use of the computer in direct instruction. (It appears that Alfred Bork's group at the University of California, Irvine, is the only other group which has produced whole physics courses involving the computer in direct instruction at the level of several

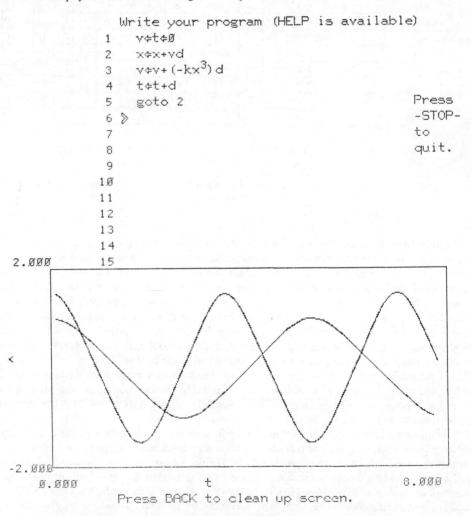

Fig. 12. The student has written a short 'grafit' program to study the oscillations of an anharmonic oscillator, then tried two different initial displacements.

hours per week [10].) Nevertheless it is worth mentioning that in addition to simulations and calculations which are simply a part of the instructional materials, we did have the students do an exercise on numerical integration using the mini-language 'grafit'. A handout explained the theory of numerical integration and showed how to create a short program as shown in Fig. 12. Various aspects of harmonic ($F = -kx$) and anharmonic ($F = -kx^3$) oscillators were explored by the students on the basis of suggested study topics, such as the effect on frequency of amplitude, mass, etc. An attractive feature of this experiment was the graphical output which is produced automatically by grafit programs.

ADMINISTRATION

Having the computer involved at such a basic level has simplified certain aspects of course administration. The on-line gradebook program automatically records students' performance on the various required PLATO activities. This has freed the instructors from the tasks of grading and keeping track of weekly homework assignments and allowed them to spend more of their time each week helping students with individual problems. It also allows the instructor to see at a glance exactly how far the students have gotten in the material and so allows him or her to plan the discussion meetings to deal with the topics the students are actually working on at the time.

Scores on the non-PLATO aspects of the course (exams, labs, etc.) are also recorded in the on-line gradebook. This greatly simplifies the task of assigning grades at the end of the course, since all the various scores are available to the computer and can be combined by whatever algorithm is decided upon. For a course with an enrollment of several hundred, this task can be quite time-consuming when done by hand. The records kept by the gradebook on an individual student are available to that student as an option on PLATO. A student can see not only his or her own scores but also a graph of the distribution of all scores showing his or her relative standing. The student can verify that the scores recorded for him or her are correct. The distribution graphs are also available and useful to the instructors and the course director.

The computer is used extensively in the course for various types of communication between the students and the teaching staff. Notices and announcements are regularly posted on PLATO; notes are sent between students and their instructors; an open 'forum' is available on-line where students can discuss their complaints, suggestions, etc.; various polls are taken to determine, for instance, conflicts with a scheduled exam time. Near the end of the semester a survey of student reaction to the course is taken on-line in such a way that anonymity is maintained, but a response (and only one response) is assured from each student.

EVALUATION

The simultaneous operation of both a traditional and a computer-based version of the course has made it possible to study the effects of introducing the computer into the course. In some cases it was possible to give the same final exam to both groups, each with over a hundred students. In every case the two groups have shown essentially the same distributions and means of the exam scores. The scores of the computer-based students are slightly higher but the difference is not statistically significant. Some longitudinal studies have also been performed by examining grades and exam scores in later physics courses and in advanced mechanics courses, for students who had the two kinds of introductory classical mechanics courses. Again no significant differences were observed. The only significant correlations noted in the longitudinal studies were that good performance in one course is strongly correlated with good performance in another course.

A pessimistic interpretation of the equivalence of the final exam scores is to say that despite the PLATO tutoring and despite the fact that almost all the PLATO students turned in all the homework problems (whereas it is known that in the non-PLATO course most students, in fact, do not do many of the assigned homework problems), nevertheless the PLATO students could not do any better on the final exam. An optimistic interpretation of the result is to say that although the PLATO students had only one lecture a week, although the discussion class was essentially taken over by PLATO (but with an instructor present to handle questions), and although the average student only spent two non-scheduled PLATO hours of study per week in this difficult course, nevertheless the PLATO students did as well on the final exam as the non-PLATO students. A realistic interpretation might be that it has always been almost impossible to see differential effects on final exams resulting from differentials in the form of instruction, at least in cases such as these. The final exam consisted of problems to be solved, not formulas to be remembered, so the exam to some extent is a test of intelligence and not just of learning. There seem to be few examples in higher education where large effects on examination scores have been observed following changes in teaching techniques when

34 D. KANE and B. SHERWOOD

dealing with such subject material. Comparisons between self-paced and traditional courses have been published[11], but of the interpretable comparisons, only one is in physics[12], and careful study of this paper shows that the supposed difference depends critically on only one or two data points, and the sample is very small.

Within the PLATO course, various correlations have been examined, such as exam scores vs homework problems completed or exam scores vs instructional lessons completed. The only significant correlations that have ever shown up have been between one exam and another. That is, if the student does well on the first exam, he or she will almost certainly do well on the second, third, and final exams. The issue is somewhat muddied by the fact that in recent semesters few students failed to turn in *all* the assigned lessons and homework, so that there is little spread to correlate against. However, these results also obtained in earlier semesters, before game or point incentives for keeping up-to-date, when at the time an exam was taken many students had not yet turned in work supposedly relevant to that exam.

Since the exam problems are quite similar to the homework problems, one would expect that doing the homework problems should help in taking an exam. However, the student can get help on the homework problems, whereas during the closed-book exam the student is completely alone, under time pressure, and facing new problems. The course therefore really has two rather different components: weekly assigned work (lab reports, PLATO lessons, and PLATO homework) and exams, the latter differing from the former in being a different kind of measurement of the student's work. We believe the weekly assigned work is just as important as the exams, even if we cannot measure by exam all aspects of the benefits of the weekly work. It is also true that a student who performs well on one component and poorly on the other will be given a passing grade. Only if the student performs poorly on both course components will he or she fail the course.

While it was convenient to correlate exams and homework in the PLATO course, given that the data were all on-line, it seems likely that the lack of correlation between these two activities is not limited to computer-based courses but is an effect which would hold true in any similar physics course.

It might also be pointed out that the PLATO course shares some aspects of 'self-paced' or 'personalized' instruction. The course is divided into modules of instruction, and mastery-level performance is required on lessons and homework to pass from one module to the next (except that students are permitted to move ahead without mastery if they get too far behind, but they do normally go back and complete the work later). If it were not for the four exams, which destroy our illusions, we would give almost all students the grade of 'A', since almost all students do, in fact, complete modules on time at a mastery level.

We have regularly asked students for their assessments of the computer-based course. Of the various questions asked, the most important to us is one which asks whether the student would prefer to take the next course in the physics sequence in a computer-based or traditional form, if both were available. The percentage of students who would choose the computer-based course has fluctuated from a low of 50% to a high of 65%. The lack of reproducibility seems to be due to non-computer aspects of the course. That is, during one semester there were many complaints about the content and grading of the exams, and student unhappiness with that component of the course spilled over into their perception of the course as a whole, so that their preference had little to do with whether the course was computer-based or not. It seems likely that the favorable responses represent a lower bound on the true situation for similar reasons: this is a very difficult course for many students, and lacking a comparable survey in the non-PLATO class we do not know how many of the preferences for a different kind of course really reflect general unhappiness with a calculus-oriented introductory mechanics course rather than unhappiness with the computer aspects.

Another important questionnaire item asked which version of the course took more total time. Semester after semester, independent of various changes in the computer-based materials (such as whether there was help available for the homework problems), 80% of the students say that the computer-based version of the course takes more of their time. This seems a curious result from the standpoint of those hours we can account for, since we have seen that on the average the students spend only 1 h studying at a terminal outside the contact hours of the non-PLATO course. Of course we do not know how much time is spent on book study, but there are indications that this is not large. Perhaps the discrepancy between student perceptions of the time spent and our own partial measurements of this time are due to the fact that terminal study is very intense and interactive, and it also requires more planning than textbook study, since there are no terminals in the student residences. On a cold winter's night it is no fun to trudge across campus to get to a terminal.

Acknowledgements—James Smith made up the homework problems and gave invaluable advice and support throughout the project. In addition to writing computer-based materials in other areas of physics, Carol

Bennett wrote several mechanics lessons and assisted in the course. While lecturing in the course, David Sutton provided guidance and wrote some materials. Graduate students Lynell Cannell, Joan Mitchell, and Charlene Thompson helped develop pilot materials on the PLATO III system. Graduate students who rewrote PLATO III materials to run on the PLATO IV system and wrote new materials included Dan Beece, Craig Burson, Thomas Lemberger, Bradley Peterson, and Charles Schultz.

REFERENCES

1. Smith S. and Sherwood B. A., *Science* **192**, 344 (1976); Sherwood B.A., *Proceedings of a Conference on Innovation and Productivity in Higher Education*. Carnegie-Mellon University, Pittsburgh (1976).
2. Sherwood B. A., Bennett C., Tenczar C. and Mitchell J., *Proceedings of a Conference on Computers in the Undergraduate Curricula*, p. 463. Dartmouth College, Hanover, NH (1971).
3. Bennett C. D., *Proceedings of a Conference on Computers in the Undergraduate Curricula*, p. 369. Southern Regional Education Board, Atlanta (1972); Bennett C. D., *Am. J. Phys.* **41**, 135 (1973).
4. Peterson S. B., Lemberger T. R. and Smith J. H., *Proceedings of a Conference on Computers in the Undergraduate Curricula*. Washington State University, Seattle, (1974).
5. Sherwood B. A., *Two-Dimensional Kinematics* (*Okinem3*). Control Data Corporation (written 1975, published 1978).
6. Sherwood B. A., *The TUTOR Language*. Control Data Corporation, Minneapolis, MN (1977); Sherwood B. A. *Am. Phys.* **40**, 1042 (1972); Sherwood B. A., *Communications of the ACM* **21**, 876 (1978).
7. Kane D., Smith J. H. and Sherwood B. A., *Problem Set: Dynamics* (*Omechhw7*). Control Data Corporation (written 1974, 1977; published 1978); Sherwood B. A., *Am. J. Phys.* **39**, 1199 (1971).
8. Sherwood B. A., *Stored Energy: The Work-Energy Equation* (*Owork*). Control Data Corporation (written 1977, published 1978).
9. Erlichson H., *Am. J. Phys.* **45**, 769 (1977); Penchina C. M., *Am. J. Phys.* **46**, 295 (1978).
10. Bork A., "Effective computer use in physics education". *Am. J. Phys.* **43**, 81 (1975).
11. Taveggia T. C., *Am. J. Phys.* **44**, 1028 (1976).
12. Austin S. M. and Gilbert E. K., *Am. J. Phys.* **41**, 12 (1973).

APPENDIX

PLATO lessons developed for the course

Title, file name, completion time, authors, and year of creation (and major revision) are shown. These lessons were published in 1978 by Control Data Corporation under the file names shown.

Introduction to PLATO for science students 25 min (Kane, 1976)	(0introduce)
Introduction to Vectors 45 min (Sherwood, 1973, 1974)	(0show)
The Vector Olympics open-ended (Sherwood, 1976)	(0vgame)
Problem set: vectors 80 min (Smith, Kane, Sherwood, 1974, 1977)	(0mechhwl)
One-dimensional kinematics (part 1) 40 min (Sherwood, Peterson, Beece, 1970, 1972, 1977)	(0kineml)
One-dimensional kinematics (part 2) 85 min (Sherwood, Beece, 1973, 1977)	(0kinem2)
Problem set: one-dimensional kinematics 70 min (Smith, Kane, Sherwood, 1974, 1977)	(0mechhw2)
Two-dimensional kinematics 140 min (Sherwood, 1975)	(0kinem3)
Problem set: two-dimensional kinematics 90 min (Smith, Kane, Sherwood, 1974, 1977)	(0mechhw3)
Forces and free-body diagrams 70 min (Bennett, 1975)	(0cb10)
Free-body diagrams 85 min (Sherwood, Burson, 1971, 1972)	(0freel)
Problem set: force and simple dynamics 85 min (Smith, Kane, Sherwood, 1974, 1977)	(0mechhwl5)
Problem set: dynamics 110 min (Smith, Kane, Sherwood, 1974, 1977)	(0mechhw7)
Work and kinetic energy 70 min (Kane, 1975)	(0dz)
Work and position-dependent forces 20 min (Kane, 1975)	(0kanel)
Problem set: work and kinetic energy 70 min (Smith, Kane, Sherwood, 1974, 1977)	(0mechhw8)
Stored energy: the work-energy equation 85 min (Sherwood, 1977)	(0work)
Problem set: conservation of energy 85 min (Smith, Kane, Sherwood, 1974, 1977)	(0mechhw16)

Conservation of momentum   (0conserve)
    45 min (Sherwood, Kane, Schultz, 1971, 1974)
Exercise on conservation of momentum   (0collide)
    open-ended (Kane, 1976)
Relative Motion   (0relmo)
    20 min (Bennett, 1975)
Relative Motion–River Problem   (0river)
    20 min (Bennett, 1973)
Finding the center of mass (particles)   (0kane)
    open-ended (Kane, 1976)
Problem set: relative motion and momentum   (0mechhwl17)
    70 min (Smith, Kane, Sherwood, 1974, 1977)
Problem set: momentum and collisions   (0mechhwl8)
    75 min (Smith, Kane, Sherwood, 1974, 1977)
Overview of rotational dynamics   (0rotdyn)
    80 min (Sherwood, 1977)
Torque and angular momentum   (0torque)
    50 min (Sherwood, 1974)
Kinetic energy of rotation, moment of inertia   (0re14)
    20 min (Kane, 1976)
Olympic games involving torque   (0torgame)
    open-ended (Bennett, 1976)
Problem set: rotational dynamics   (0mechhw10)
    65 min (Smith, Kane, Sherwood, 1974, 1977)
Free-body diagrams with rotations   (0free2)
    65 min (Sherwood, Burson, 1972, 1973)
Problem set: rotation problems   (0mechhw11)
    80 min (Smith, Kane, Sherwood, 1974, 1977)
Problem set: torque and angular momentum   (0mechhw12)
    80 min (Smith, Kane, Sherwood, 1974, 1977)
Oscillations: simple harmonic motion   (0oscill)
    100 min (Sherwood, 1974)
Problem set: simple harmonic motion   (0mechhwl4)
    50 min (Smith, Kane, Sherwood, 1974, 1977)
Gravitational potential energy   (0gravpot)
    115 min (Beece, 1978)
Problem set: gravitation   (0mechhwl3)
    60 min (Smith, Kane, Sherwood, Beece 1974, 1977)
Phizquiz: a problem-solving test   (0phizquizl)
    50 min (Peterson, 1973)
An interterminal problem-solving contest   (0p106conl)
    open-ended (Kane, 1976)
Physics games   (0physgame)
    open-ended (Bennett, 1975)
grafit (a mini-programming language)   (0grafit)
    open-ended (Sherwood, 1971)

Comput. & Educ., Vol. 4, pp. 37 to 57
Pergamon Press Ltd 1980. Printed in Great Britain

PHYSICS IN THE IRVINE EDUCATIONAL TECHNOLOGY CENTER

A. BORK

University of California, Irvine

This paper reviews the physics learning material produced by the Physics Computer Development Project at the University of California, Irvine. This project is part of the recently formed Educational Technology Center. The work discussed has been supported by the National Science Foundation and the University of California for eleven years.

The discussion is divided into four sections. The first concerns our most complete development of a course involving computers, the first quarter of a beginning mechanics course. The second section concerns development of computer-based learning materials in other parts of physics. The third section reviews the production strategies which have evolved at Irvine, a critical part of the process of producing efficient and effective material. Finally, the fourth section concerns the future of computer-based learning in physics and other areas.

THE MECHANICS QUARTER

As with many of the early computer-based learning projects we began producing individual programs where the computer could play a role in aiding students. After some years, we became interested in the problem of creating an entire quarter. With support from a National Science Foundation grant for this purpose, we set out to restructure a beginning physics quarter, developing a variety of learning materials in addition to those employing the computer. The restructured quarter was first taught in the winter of 1976 to pre-medical students. It was evaluated by a group headed by Michael Scriven and revised.

The most recent presentation in January 1979 was to a group of science and engineering majors. In this last instance, the computer-based format was optional, offered along with a course taught in a standard fashion. Approximately half the students, about 200, opted for the computer-based version. These students used over 10,000 on-line programs in the ten week quarter, consuming over 5000 terminal hours of computer time on Irvine's Honeywell Sigma 7 timesharing system. The displays were Tektronix 4013s.

The following objectives stimulated the development of the course. (a) The course should be acceptable to physics faculty members as a beginning quarter in physics. This precluded an extremely experimental course and suggested a course somewhat like the existing beginning courses. (b) The materials should provide as great a degree of individualized assistance to students as possible. (c) Students should be offered as many options as possible, including options in *pacing*, in *learning materials*, and in *content*. (d) The computer was to be only one of a variety of learning modes. (e) The course was to go through several cycles of modification, based on student response to the materials. (f) The computer was to be used in a variety of modes, allowing different possibilities for different students. (g) No initial philosophical decisions were made about one way of employing the computer. (h) The course should assume students with a wide variety of backgrounds, not making the usual assumptions about a homogeneous student group. (i) The materials were to employ graphic capabilities wherever they aided in the learning process. We believe that graphics is an important part of the learning process, particularly with students who are not the most verbally apt students.

Easy transportability to many machines was *not* one of the goals of this development. Rather, attempts at making programs so that they could run on many machines would, we felt, only lead to less effective pedagogical material. The project developers felt that transportability should not be the major issue at this early stage in the development of computer-based learning material. We argued that these problems would be solved by later technology. Our position has been vindicated by recent developments, as will be discussed in the last section of this paper.

The course designers were Alfred Bork and Joseph Marasco. Stephen Franklin played a major role in the development of the on-line quizzes. A group of excellent student programmers worked under the direction of Estelle Warner.

COURSE STRUCTURE

We chose a Keller plan or personalized system of instruction format for the course. Three reasons guided this choice: the reported effectiveness of this process as compared with other modes of learning, its greater flexibility, and the special role we felt computers could play in the process.

The use of a personalized system of instruction in physics and other areas had been well tested before this project. Various research reports have indicated that this system is effective as compared with usual fixed-pace, lecture-based courses. We did not, however, approach this as "true believers'; we were willing to adapt the structures of PSI to meet our needs.

A brief review of the developmental process may be useful for those not familiar with such a way of offering a course. Course material is divided into units. Each unit has a description which states carefully the objectives of the unit, reviews the learning modes available, and offers sample unit tests. Preparation of the unit tests, a careful match to the objectives explicitly described to the students, is the next major step in developing the course. Then additional learning materials are produced.

The usual stance of a PSI course is that students may not take tests in a unit until they have completed tests for previous units. The student should have 'mastered' the material before proceeding. This means several versions of each unit test must be available, since the student will retake the test if he or she has not performed perfectly.

The majority of courses of this kind involve little or no computer material. Indeed, there seems to be a 'tradition' with PSI courses that the only acceptable learning material is textbook or note material; this tradition was not followed in the course being described.

In the first year of offering the course we discovered that our major bottleneck was in giving the unit tests. We offered these during this initial year in the usual written form, graded by teaching assistants. The department was unable to supply enough teaching assistants to cover the 300 students in the course adequately. We often had long lines in the testing room. Students complained, probably with justification, that different teaching assistants graded the unit tests differently. When we investigated how others were handling this situation we discovered that our problems were common.

This led us into the development of a complete set of on-line exams. These quizzes have now been used for three separate uses of the course. There are 27 exams for the mechanics material, used in the structure to be described. Usually several tests had to be passed by the students for each unit.

STRUCTURE OF THIS COURSE

One of our purposes was to offer students choice of *content*. Hence, we developed several 'tracks' for students to pursue. The number of tracks has varied for different offerings of the course from 2 to 6. Two fundamentally different sets of materials were available; the greater number of choices is based on crossovers between the two sets of units.

PHYSICS 5A		Course 2		Winter 1978 UCI
Unit	Chapters	Quizzes	Dialogs	Bonus point Date
2.1	1, 2 3 (to p. 52)	Slope Vectors		January 16
2.2	Rest of 3	Projectile Pop	Circle	January 23
2.3	4, 5	Newt	Motion Blows	January 30
2.4	6	Com Impulse	Momentum Hockey	February 6
2.5	7	Nrg Forpot Twobody	Conserve Work Pot (optional unit)	February 13
2.6	10, 11, 12	Rotkin Rotdyn1 Rotdyn2	Circle Rotation	February 20 (Holiday)
2.7	13 (to p. 378)	Pend Spring	Motion Harmonic	February 27
2.8	Rest of 13	Damp	Motion Harmonic Couposc	March 6

PHYSICS 5A   Course 3   Winter 1978 UCI

Unit	Quizzes	Dialogs	Bonus Point Date
3.1	Accel Move Eqar	Blows	January 16
3.2	Apluse Aplexp (APL workspace) Aplprog (APL workspace)	Aplp	January 23
3.3	Ho Slope	Motion	January 30
3.4	Grav	Motion	February 6
3.5	Pot Forpot	Conserve	February 13
3.6	Mom Pop	Momentum Hockey	February 20 (Holiday)
3.7	Damp	Harmonic	February 27
3.8	Coup	Couposc	March 6

One track is based on a standard beginning textbook, and so resembles the beginning quarter physics taught at most colleges. Several textbooks have been used, with only minor modification in the course structure; all existing popular books are similar.

The alternate track was based on a set of notes developed by the author, initially at Reed College and more recently at the University of California, Irvine. These notes assume that the students will be using the computer as a *programming* device as well as in other ways. This approach to mechanics arrives quickly at $F = ma$ as a differential equation, using numerical techniques to allow students to solve the equation. The notes are kept in computer readable form and have been updated several times; xeroxed versions are sold to the students.

Most units have several tests, taken in any order. As with any PSI course students take the test a number of times, until they show understanding of the concepts of that unit. Here is a list of quizzes in the two tracks as used in winter 1979.

Since students must make choices early in the course some consideration goes into course descriptions that aid them in choosing both content and learning modes. While for some students choice of content is important, for others little thought is given to the process. The same literature presses students to pick a conscious strategy for pacing themselves through the course. A variety of strategies are discussed. The object is to make the student aware of the possibilities so that he or she does not simply drift. We take a number of steps to counteract procrastination; we do not find it a serious problem within our course.

We summarize the student's role in the course by means of flowchart.

THE ON-LINE TESTS

The heart of the course is the on-line tests which students repeat until they demonstrate that they have mastered the objectives of the unit. These tests are not only tests, but provide detailed aid to the students. Thus they serve as one of the major learning components of the course.

Since they are critical in such a course, I describe two tests in detail to illustrate the different structures of these tests. One of the tests shown in SLOPE, used in the beginning of the quarter while the other test, COUP, is used at the end of the quarter. SLOPE is used in both tracks of the course, but COUP is used only in the 'computer' track.

As with all our quizzes, SLOPE begins (Fig. 1) with a title page which gives a brief description of the contents of the quiz and gives the names of the authors.

The introductory frame to the quiz (Fig. 2) describes the content in more detail and also offers the student a help sequence.

These help sequences are *not* part of the quiz. The quizzes have a forty minute maximum, but the time spent in the help sequence does not count toward this. Nor does it count as an instance of taking the quiz. We follow a sequence in which the student does *not* request the help sequence.

The SLOPE quiz starts with two simple objectives concerning mathematical background. The first is, 'Can a student read a graph?' and the second is, 'Can a student put a point on the graph?' The

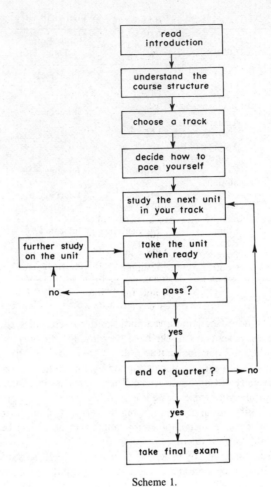

Scheme 1.

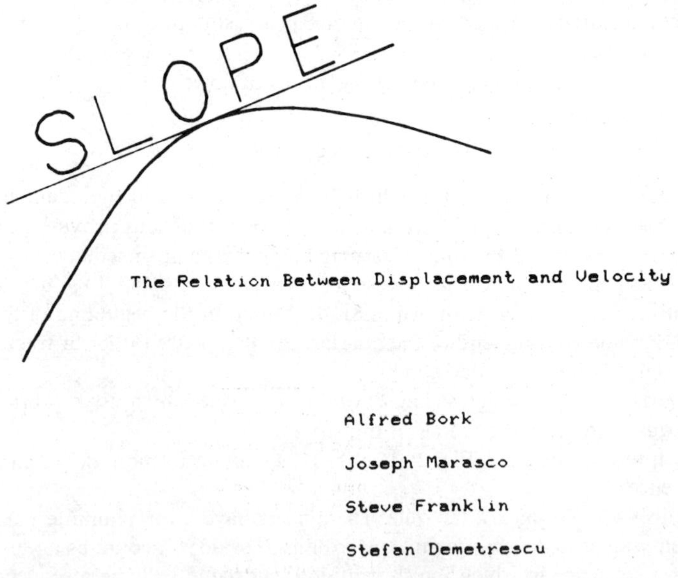

SLOPE

The Relation Between Displacement and Velocity

Alfred Bork

Joseph Marasco

Steve Franklin

Stefan Demetrescu

Fig. 1.

```
    The purpose of this dialog is to check your
understanding of the graphical relationship
between displacement, velocity and acceleration.
for one dimensional mechanical systems.


    We are prepared to offer you some help with this.
topic before quizzing you.

        Would you like this help?
```

Fig. 2.

curves and the data are randomly picked within specifications provided by the authors. Figure 3 shows a question and the computer's response to a successful student input.

The next objective is to see if students can identify the points of *zero velocity* on a graph of displacement versus time. The built-in crosshairs are employed. In the sequence illustrated (Fig. 4) the student has identified one point correctly, then pointed to a place where the *position* was zero rather than the velocity, prompting the detailed aid given, then pointed to another correct position, then claimed that he or she had pointed to them all, and then, finally, under prodding by the computer, pointed to the third (and last) value with a zero velocity. Figure 4 shows this series of interactions between the student and the computer, all on one screen.

Two successive questions then investigate whether the student can identify on the position-time curve where the velocity is positive and where it is negative. Since this curve will be different each

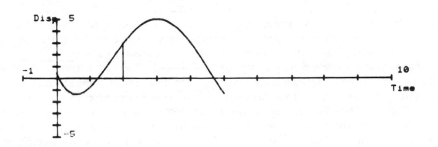

```
What is the position at time 2? 3

Correct
```

Fig. 3.

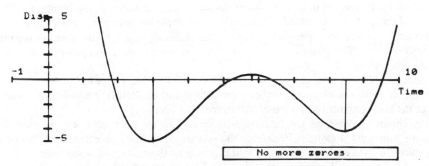

```
Here is the displacement-time curve.

Point to times where the velocity is zero,
or point to the box that says "no more zeroes".

    You are not distinguishing between
velocity zero and position zero.
    Have another go at it.
That's not all there are.  Look a bit harder.
```

Fig. 4.

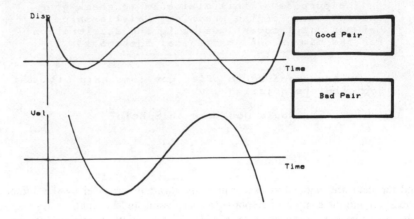

Yes, they don't go together.

PRESS RETURN TO CONTINUE

Fig. 5.

time the quiz is run, and since various positive and negative parts occur, the computer must determine which answers are correct. As with all the other questions asked in our quizzes, students receive immediate appropriate response for a correct or incorrect answer.

The next two sequences are the main parts of the quiz. They use a strategy, developed by Stephen Franklin of Irvine, called concealed multiple choice. First, the machine generates a 'question'. In this case the question is a position-time curve. The curve is generated randomly following the authors' specifications. Then the computer generates right and wrong possible velocity time curves. These are displayed to the student *one-by-one* in a random order. Thus, the student may immediately be shown a correct position-velocity pair or may go through six or so attempts before receiving a correct one. For each such pair a student *must* assert whether that pair is correct or not. Figure 5 shows one picture from such a sequence.

The process is repeated for the velocity acceleration combination. Figure 6 illustrates what happens when a student claims that a velocity curve is correct, when it is not.

SLOPE concludes with a question based on a velocity time curve and asks for information about position.

As a second example of a quiz, I consider COUP, concerned with coupled oscillators. This quiz is at the end of the quarter in one track. It is an advanced topic for beginning courses, showing that the computer approach can bring people more quickly to difficult physics. Figure 7 shows the title frame.

The introduction (Fig. 8) shows details about the quiz and offers computer-based learning aids before the quiz is entered.

For each use of the quiz a new problem is generated. Two basic types of problems are provided. The computer picks one of these two types randomly, and then picks the values of masses and the values of the spring constants randomly within specified limits.

After preliminary questions the first major issue is whether the student can identify the correct Newtonian equations of motions describing the system. Again the concealed multiple choice format plays a role. For each equation of motion that is presented the student must say whether it is or is not a correct description of the system. As with other examples of this kind, many correct answers are possible, and the student must identify the correct form. Unlike printed multiple choice quizzes the students cannot answer the question correctly merely by eliminating bad guesses. Figure 9 shows a student rejecting an incorrect response.

The program distinguishes between two different types of incorrect responses—ones where students have made a sign error in the forces and ones in which the problems are deeper. In the first case the student is told to be more careful with signs and is continued. Once again the computer can give detailed assistance to a student in difficulty.

Disp
Good Pair
Time
Point to one!
Bad Pair
Vel
Time
Vel
No. Here is the right curve.
Time
PRESS RETURN TO CONTINUE...

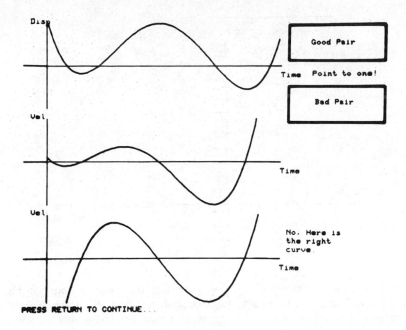

Fig. 6.

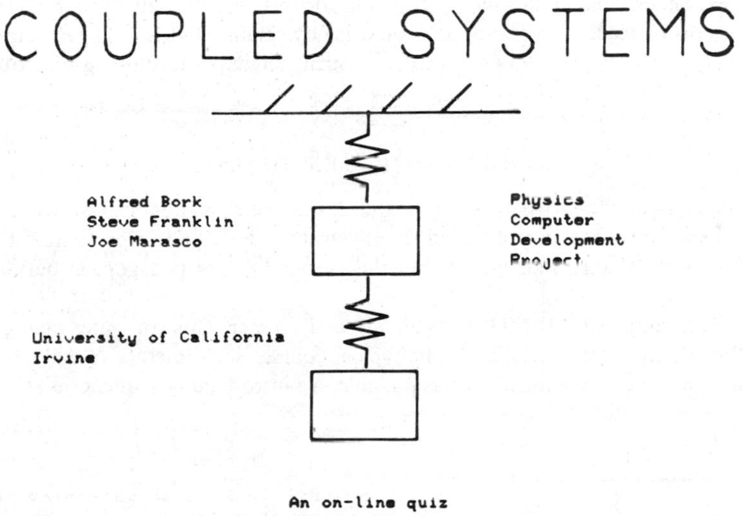

COUPLED SYSTEMS
Alfred Bork
Steve Franklin
Joe Marasco
Physics
Computer
Development
Project
University of California
Irvine
An on-line quiz

Fig. 7.

This quiz concerns the equations of motion, the characteristic frequencies, and the normal modes of a coupled oscillatory system. You'll need pencil and paper.

A dialog, COUPOSC, is available for reviewing these concepts. Would you like to review or to proceed directly to the quiz?
?

Fig. 8.

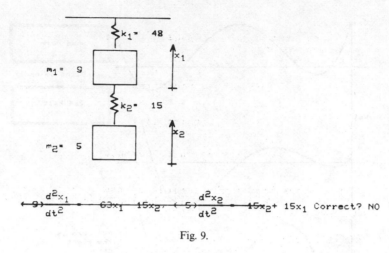

Fig. 9.

The next stage is to identify the characteristic frequencies of the system, as shown in Fig. 10.

If a student has difficulties, we backtrack. The characteristic frequencies come in their final state through solutions of a quadratic equation. We get students who are having difficulties to identify the components of this quadratic equation to see if that is the stage of the problem in which troubles are occurring. It is sometimes possible to break a major problem up into a series of pieces in this fashion and so isolate the problem. If we were interested only in quizzing we would not do this, but, we stress, the quiz is an intimate blend of testing and learning.

These two examples, among the many available, do not exhaust all the strategies used in the quizzes. The interested reader can best appreciate these by running quizzes. The examples should give some flavor of the process even though they miss such details as the timing and other interactive aspects.

OTHER COMPUTER DIALOGS

Both the students and the instructors see the quizzes as the most important learning material. But other learning experiences are also provided. To illustrate. I describe two programs. These programs are related; they both concern momentum, but they serve different pedagogical purposes within the course.

One of these programs, MOMENTUM, is an *interactive proof*. This computer dialog considers one of the major 'bread and butter' derivations of a typical course. Such interactive dialogs try to lead the students to 'discover' the derivations as far as possible. An introductory sequence is shown in Fig. 11.

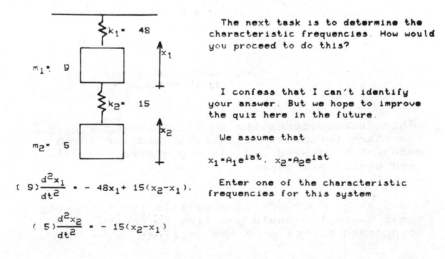

Fig. 10.

```
Three aspects of the physics of moving bodies
are of concern to us:


      1. Newton's second law.


      2. Newton's third law.


      3. Conservation of momentum.


We'll investigate the logical connections between these
three.  Our conclusion will be that they are logically
interdependent.
```

Press RETURN to continue...

Fig. 11.

The logical relations being investigated are those between Newton's second and third laws and conservation of momentum. Proofs are generated in both directions. The program starts by checking the student's knowledge of the background laws needed, as in Fig. 12, concerning the way Newton's third law works.

Several typical frames from later in the dialog are shown in Figs 13, 14, 15 and 16.

An entirely different approach is used in HOCKEY. A laboratory environment is simulated, as if the student had the ability to do many 'experiments.' These involve three different types of one- and two-dimensional collisions of pucks. The student is pressed to generalize on observed data and is given help if this turns out to be difficult (See Fig. 17).

INTUITION

An important goal in our course is to develop student intuition. This task has not proved easy. The full description of our trials and tribulations will not be given; the reader is referred to other available papers.

The principal program in the mechanics quarter intended to build intuition is a program developed many years ago by the author and Richard Ballard, MOTION. This dialog allows an easy way for the student to 'play' with mechanical systems, changing the initial conditions, the force laws, the constants in the force laws, and the curves plotted. Unlike many of our programs, MOTION is not easy for the beginner to use; a one page printed introduction is available. .

```
      Now let's take a look at Newton's third law;
sometimes called the law of action and reaction.
```

```
When two objects act on each other, the forces on
each due to the other are of equal magnitude and
opposite direction.

If this is the force acting
on one object,
                                    △


                                         ...point to the tip
   △                                     of the force vector
                                         on the other object.
```

Fig. 12.

Yes, that's fine.

$$F = ma$$ The bold letters
indicate vectors

However, for the purposes of this dialog
it would be easier to use a form explicitly
involving momentum.

Can you give me such a form?

Fig. 13.

Are you familiar with the concept of momentum? YES

Good.

We are interested in the conservation of momentum.

What does it mean to say that momentum is conserved?

? IT DOES NOT CHANGE WITH TIME

That looks o.k. to me.

Conservation of momemtum means that the total
momentum of a system is constant - it doesn't change
with time.

Press RETURN to continue...

Fig. 14.

We begin by writing Newton's laws for each body.

$$^1\triangle$$

$$\triangle^2$$

$$F_1 = \frac{d}{dt} P_1 \qquad\qquad F_2 = \frac{d}{dt} P_2$$

F_1 and F_2 are the forces on each particle.

What do you want to do with these equations? ADD THEM??
That's reasonable.

Fig. 15.

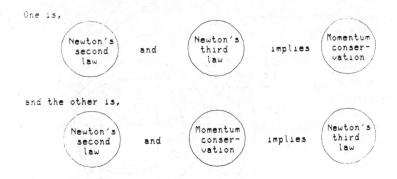

We'll pursue two proofs to show the interconections here.

One is,

Newton's second law   and   Newton's third law   implies   Momentum conservation

and the other is,

Newton's second law   and   Momentum conservation   implies   Newton's third law

In the process we'll also consider some interesting restrictions to the validity of the third law.

Press RETURN to continue...

Fig. 16.

To allow the majority of the students in the class to develop such intuition, we have found it essential to provide workbook material which guides students into interesting situations and then asks questions about these cases. (This material is available upon request.) The workbook exercises were an afterthought. In our early days of using MOTION we were highly impressed by what it could do, and many of our colleagues and visitors were also. But it became apparent that more was needed if it was to be used within classroom environments, bringing the intuitive point of view to the majority of the class. Simulations are often extremely attractive to the faculty member and to the highly motivated student, but they are not necessarily effective with the typical student. We have developed a variety of tactics to use in integrating such materials into a course structure so that they become effective learning materials.

To illustrate the procedure of using MOTION and the exercises, I show several questions asked in an exercise on gravitational motion, interspersing questions with the plots the student may see at the computer display. Students are asked to write brief descriptions for each question.

1. Logon, enter MOTION, and choose INVERSE SQUARE force. The initial PLOT is for $X = 3$, $Y = 0$, $VX = 0$, $VY = 0.5$.
2. OVERPLOT with VY values from 0·4 to 1, in steps of 0·1. Describe the results. Are there different types of orbits? (See Fig. 18.)
3. Now study the system point in *velocity space*. That is,

    PLOT   VX   VS   VY

    for the range of initial conditions suggested in 2 above. What orbits do you find? (See Fig. 19.)
4. Now you are to see what would happen if gravitational force were *not quite* inverse square. Ask for the EQUATION again; the power is N. Set

    $N = -1.9$

OUR TWO PUCKS HAVE THE FOLLOWING INITIAL VELOCITY COMPONENTS..

	PUCK A		PUCK B
	Vx = 5		Vx = -3
	Vy = 0		Vy = 0

PRESS RETURN TO BEGIN THE EXPERIMENT

Fig. 17.

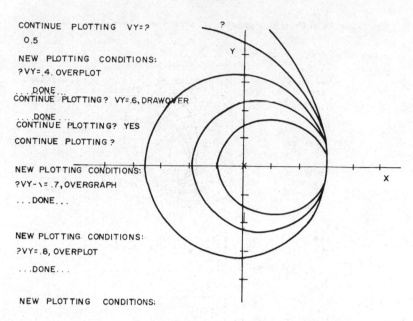

```
CONTINUE PLOTTING  VY=?
   0.5

NEW PLOTTING CONDITIONS:
?VY=.4,OVERPLOT

    DONE...
CONTINUE PLOTTING? VY=.6,DRAWOVER

 ..DONE...
CONTINUE PLOTTING? YES

CONTINUE PLOTTING?


NEW PLOTTING CONDITIONS:
?VY-\=.7,OVERGRAPH

 ...DONE...


NEW PLOTTING CONDITIONS:
?VY=.8, OVERPLOT

 ...DONE...


NEW PLOTTING  CONDITIONS:
```

Fig. 18.

Return to plotting the X–Y- space, investigating a range of values around −2. You may want to continue plotting each orbit. What can you say about the results? What happens for values less than 2? Greater than 2? (See Fig. 20.)

5. Now consider the case of *two* gravitational force centers, as if you had two *fixed* suns. Request

TWO FORCE CENTERS

at any input. The initial conditions will be reset. Determine them by typing

X, Y, VX, VY = ?

PLOT the orbit. Discuss the possibility of life on a planet with such an orbit (See Fig. 21.)

6. See if you can find velocities that give closed (repeated) orbits. What velocities do this? Sketch the orbits (See Fig. 22).

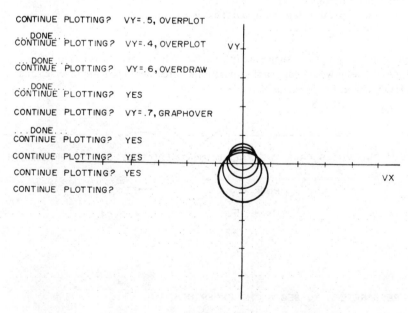

```
CONTINUE PLOTTING?   VY=.5, OVERPLOT

  ...DONE...
CONTINUE PLOTTING?   VY=.4, OVERPLOT      VY

  ...DONE...
CONTINUE PLOTTING?   VY=.6, OVERDRAW

  ...DONE...
CONTINUE PLOTTING?   YES

CONTINUE PLOTTING?   VY=.7, GRAPHOVER

  ...DONE...
CONTINUE PLOTTING?   YES

CONTINUE PLOTTING?   YES

CONTINUE PLOTTING?   YES

CONTINUE PLOTTING?
```

Fig. 19.

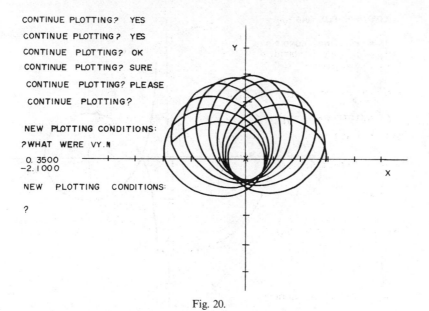

Fig. 20.

The final component of the course is the course management system. Anyone who has done bookkeeping for a large course can appreciate that a major advantage of giving all the tests on-line is that the computer can serve as the record keeper. Student records are accessible at all times, and student questions about their progress in the course can be resolved immediately by the instructor using the on-line data base. The data base needs to be designed with flexibility and security in mind.

In our case the data base was developed as a CODASYL-type data base using the EDMS capabilities of the Honeywell Sigma 7. The interface programs for the data base were primarily COBOL programs. The data base was constructed in a general way so as to cover not only PSI courses but a variety of other courses.

A particularly interesting use of the on-line data base is to alert the instructor about problems occurring in the course. Two types of problems are of interest—those with the course materials and those with student progress. Figure 23 is a histogram showing performance on one of the on-line tests. Histograms can indicate tests with trouble, if too many people have taken three or more tries to pass this particular test, as compared with the general standards for personalized system of instruction tests. The indication is that something is clearly wrong, either with the objectives, the tests, or the

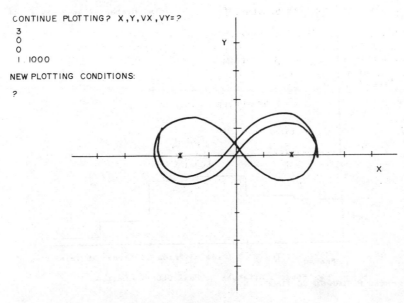

Fig. 21.

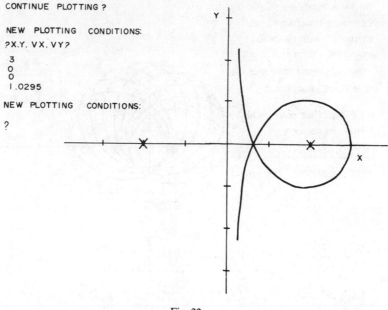

CONTINUE PLOTTING ?

NEW PLOTTING   CONDITIONS:
?X.Y. VX. VY?
   3
   0
   0
   1.0295

NEW PLOTTING   CONDITIONS:

?

Fig. 22.

learning materials. Problem areas can immediately be studied and corrected, although whether one wants to do this for the immediate course or save the correction for the next year's material is an interesting moral question.

Another application of an on-line data base is dealing with student problems. Procrastination is the first such problem, common in PSI courses generally. The fact that the data is immediately available makes it easy to spot at several stages in the course when students are behind in the activities of the course. For example, we send out a letter to each student in the class at approximately the end of the first week who has not attempted *any* on-line quizzes. The letter asks those students to see the instructor, pointing out that they should have already been active in the course. Other letters are sent at different stages.

Another way to check on student problems is in the scatter plot shown in Fig. 24. Along the horizontal axis we have plotted weeks per unit, and along the vertical axis tries per quiz. Each of the

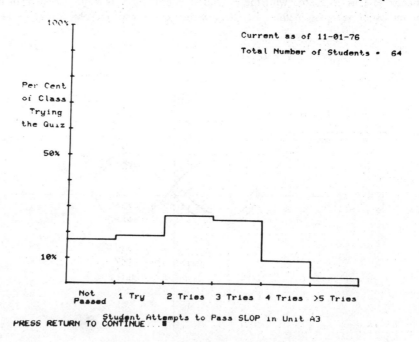

Current as of 11-01-76

Total Number of Students = 64

Per Cent
of Class
Trying
the Quiz

100%

50%

10%

Not   1 Try   2 Tries   3 Tries   4 Tries   >5 Tries
Passed

Student Attempts to Pass SLOP in Unit A3

PRESS RETURN TO CONTINUE... █

Fig. 23.

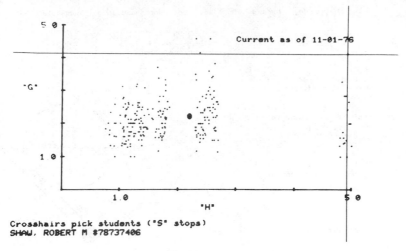

Fig. 24.

dots represents a group of students. Students can be identified by pointing to the appropriate dots. A particularly interesting group is the group in the upper left area of the graph. These students are moving through the course at a good pace, but only by doing more work than other students. They sometimes turn out to be students with poor study habits. I know of no other way of conducting a course which would have led to such an easy way to identify such students, although in principle (with a considerable amount of work) it would be possible in any PSI course.

WORK OTHER THAN THE BEGINNING PHYSICS QUARTER

In addition to the beginning physics quarter, our group at Irvine has been active in developing computer-aided learning material in other directions.

The greatest subject area of concentration other than mechanics is in electricity and magnetism. We have a range of programs in that field, including the types discussed in connection with the mechanics material. But we do not have a full quarter's work. A colleague at California State University, Dominguez Hills, Samuel Wiley, is developing areas of electricity and magnetism that we have not fully covered in our material, using similar developmental strategies to those described in the present paper.

An important aspect of our work outside of mechanics has been the dialogs authored with Arnold Arons at the University of Washington. Arons has spent two Christmas periods with us; he and the author developed six highly interactive computer-based dialogs, two in astronomy, one in thermo-dynamics, and three on magnetic fields. All of them are in the pedagogical tradition that derives from the work of Jean Piaget. They assume a student not yet fully capable of all the aspects of formal reasoning and aid that student to make progress from the concrete operational stage toward the formal operational stage. The strategy is to stay close to the phenomena, avoiding great generaliza-tions, and to move very slowly. As with other computer-based learning material, the student determines the pace and takes as much time as is necessary with as much review as is necessary. Figures 25, 26 and 27 show three examples.

We consider this problem—students not fully capable of formal reasoning—to be a major current educational problem throughout the United States. Recent studies show that about half of our college students are in this category, on both entering and leaving. Although a number of efforts are reporting success in aiding college students to attain full reasoning capabilities, these efforts are highly localized and affect only a very small percentage of the students in the country. The problem should be initially tackled at the junior high school level, where Piaget placed the transition.

Independently we began discussions some time ago with a group at California State University, Fullerton (Frank Collea) and California State University, Long Beach (Susan Nummedal), concerning the possibility of giving the Piaget-type interview directly on-line at computer displays. These examin-ations determine a student's progress in intellectual development. We have been particularly con-cerned with the transition from concrete to formal reasoning. These exams are currently under

You are probably familiar with the idea of measuring temperature in...

        — a room —
        — the outdoors —
        — your own body—
        — an oven —

What do you do to measure your own
body temperature ?
?HUH ?

What is the name of the instrument used
for this purpose ?
?A THERMOMETER

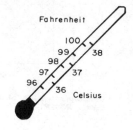

That's correct !
We need a thermometer

Please press return key to continue

Fig. 25.

Now let's take a pan of hot
water on a table...

Put a thermometer in the water...

Another thermometer is
on the wall of the room...

After a few minutes do the two
thermometers read the same ? THEY DO NOT

We agree.

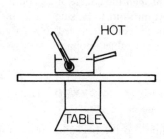

The temperature in the room doesn't change. The
wall thermometer continues to read the same

What happens to the reading on the thermometer in the hot water ? GOES DOWN

Yes. So the temperature of the water decreases.
How far does this decrease continue?

Fig. 26.

Consider another situation with the same initial and final
temperatures, but again where something different happens
along the way

Take two containers of water...

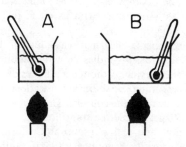

One has more water than
the other...

Suppose we put identical
burners under each...

Each has a thermometer...

Both containers start at
20 degrees C. and are
raised to 80 degrees...

Which gets to 80 degrees first ? A

Fig. 27.

preparation. We expect them to provide a more uniform assessment of cognitive development than the interviews and a more flexible testing procedure than the written forms of the exams.

The Irvine group is undertaking several small joint activities with the Irvine Unified School District in our immediate vicinity. Although most of our work thus far has been with postsecondary education, we are therefore actively considering directions in other components of education.

We regard an important component of education to be the education of the general populace either through home study mechanisms or through such institutions as public libraries, science museums, shopping centers, and airport areas. Public understanding of science is a particularly important aspect of such education. So far almost no highly interactive computer modules have been developed for these environments. We are developing learning quizzes for such public environments to gain further experience with the computer as a learning device for students who are not in formal educational institutions.

AUTHORING CONSIDERATIONS

In our work computer-based learning materials we have been particularly concerned about an effective *authoring process* or system. By an authoring or production system, I mean the process of beginning with ideas and ending with tested computer-based learning material—the entire process.

Earlier work with computer-based learning material was based on what might be termed the 'Coursewriter strategy,' employed by IBM and others in the early days of the Coursewriter project. Similar strategies have motivated many other projects. Plato, in its University of Illinois realization, used a similar strategy. The idea was like this. First, an authoring language was developed and made widely available to interested faculty. (Such authoring languages were often based on rather limited views of the full range of capabilities of computer-based learning material, particularly in the early days when the possibilities were not fully understood.) The second stage in this process was to teach faculty members to use this language, hopefully briefly. The third stage would be that the faculty member would prepare computer-based learning materials, programming directly in the language.

The Coursewriter strategy seemed inadequate to us at the onset. The languages developed, although simple for the professional programmer, were seldom simple for the uninitiated faculty. Often these languages did not provide graphic capabilities; they proved to be precrustean beds for the author's ideas. A faculty member might, with effort, learn the rudiments of a language such as Coursewriter, Pilot or Tutor, but then would proceed to write rather simpleminded material, because that was all that was possible with his or her programming capability at that stage. If a faculty member had the persistence to stay with a project for a long time and so learn the language fully, very good material might be produced. But examination of projects using this approach shows that was seldom the situation. The materials produced by faculty with long-range association were often the backbone of demonstrations to convince the beginning faculty to try this approach. Thus, in the Plato system the elegant chemistry materials developed by Stan Smith, the product of years of close association with the system, were often displayed.

If sizable numbers of very good teachers are to be involved in developing computer-based materials, other strategies must be followed. Many excellent teachers have no interest in learning a programming language and spending hours at displays inputting information. The intercept between good teachers and even potentially good programmers is a much smaller set than the set of good teachers.

The Irvine criteria for developing authoring capabilities are as follows:

1. The authoring system should allow as many extremely good teachers to be involved as possible.

2. The author or authors should be free to make any desirable pedagogical decisions; they should not be restricted in any way in their choices. We recognize that different authors may have very different pedagogical styles and might develop programs with various purposes in mind.

3. The authoring system should not require teachers to learn a programming language.

4. The authoring system should have training aspects which introduce good teachers to the capabilities of the new learning medium, the computer, in assisting learning.

5. Graphics is a critical part of the learning process and should be an option available to the instructor at all stages.

6. The instructor's mode of working should not be too different from the modes he or she is already familiar with from other media.

7. The material displayed on the screen, both text and graphics, should be formatted to be as appealing as possible to the student, using the unique capabilities of the computer.

8. The product of the faculty members should be in such a form that it can be given directly to a production team.

9. The production team should include both programmers and graphic designers, and the production method should involve some interface between these individuals.

10. Software should be provided to enable the graphic designer, coming from conventional print media or industrial design background, to work in a way that is as natural as possible for such a person.

11. The programming capabilities employed should lend themselves to large complex programs as the eventual products are often very complex. These capabilities should encourage the best contemporary programming practices.

12. The final program should be well documented, in terms of both actual comments embedded in a program and self-documentation provided by the language itself.

13. The program should be easily modifiable by programmers who did not initially work on it to effect needed improvements.

14. Feedback from student use is an essential part of the developmental process. Several rounds of using the program with students and improving it are needed before the program is considered to be 'finished'.

One important aspect of this production strategy is that we assume that a number of individuals may be involved in developing the material. The situation is analogous to that of book production. An author or authors will be responsible for the initial manuscript. At that stage a variety of people—editors, artists, graphic designers, typesetters and printing press operators—prepare the author's specifications for the final product. No one suggests that an author of books should learn how to run a printing press, analogous to the Coursewriter strategy where the author was expected to carry out the entire process.

It we are to develop sizable amounts of computer-based learning material, careful consideration needs to be given to an authoring process which will be both efficient in terms of costs and which will produce the most effective learning materials.

Our own realization of the authoring system, following these criteria, has recently undergone evolution. I describe both the old authoring system and a newer one we are currently developing. The old authoring system was developed primarily for the timesharing environment while the newer one is working primarily on stand-alone machines at the present time. We expect the newer authoring structures, even though the *target machines* (the ones the students' use) will be stand-alone machines, to run eventually on more extensive computer capabilities.

The first stage of any full curriculum development in any sizable component of a course must begin with the overall design of the material. The process is like that of any good instructional design process. Choice of overall methods, media selection mechanisms, the immediate objectives and the deeper underlying objectives, must all be chosen. This process is described elsewhere.

The critical place to begin developing a good learning environment is with a good teacher. Our experience indicates that much better material is generated when teachers work in groups of two or three rather than as single individuals or in larger groups. A single individual misses many of the components of the eventual student-computer dialog. That is, one person's experience with students is usually not sufficient to suggest a full range of alternate possibilities for student replies and learning approaches to match these replies. Several people working together pool experiences and produce a better product. But increased effectiveness of the dialogs must be weighed against the increased cost when several people are involved.

The group must be congenial, and each individual willing to compromise. An individual who believes that only one way to do anything is reasonable, not willing to listen to arguments from colleagues, will not function well in this environment. A large group leads to endless pedagogical debates, cutting down considerably on the amount of material produced.

Our authors produce materials in what might be described as a rough flowchart form. No formal flowchart training is undertaken or is necessary; the term 'flowchart' may not even be used! The developmental process is viewed by the teachers as a pedagogical process. What information is to be displayed to the student, both graphic and verbal? How is this information to be displayed? What questions are to be asked? What student replies are to be responded to? How many attempts will be given on a particular question? What kind of aid is to be offered to a student who has an identifiable problem? How many times is aid to be offered? All these we regard as learning issues, not computer issues. This list is far from exhaustive.

New faculty are typically trained within the process itself. In a group of two or three one person may be completely 'new'. That person will already have examined a good many computer-based learning materials with knowledgeable people, examining the possibilities of the medium. They learn to do flowcharting by seeing others in the group do it. The task seems natural to most teachers. No programming is involved.

It is not necessary or desirable to do this work within a typical school environment. It is better to escape from interruptions to pleasant locations for the work. Many of our best materials have been written beside swimming pools and jacuzzis. Large sheets of paper, avoiding much cross referencing between pages, are effective in producing instructional descriptions, but we have also worked with ordinary paper.

The authors may or may not want to specify in detail how the material is to be displayed on the screen. Pedagogical considerations are involved, and some authors have strong views about such issues. If the authors wish, they can draw sketches of the screen indicating where things are to be placed, both text and graphics.

Some common pitfalls exist, particularly for beginning authors. Authors may view the screen as a replacement for paper. Beginning authors particularly accustomed to textbook or lecture environments, tend to write noninteractive materials with the student playing a passive role. In most cases this tendency can be overcome by the persistence of the other members of the authoring group.

The implementation of the material produced by the production group should involve a variety of people with different types of skills. All of the following *processes* might be involved, but not necessarily with separate individuals carrying out each.

An increasingly important stage in text production these days is the editorial stage. Editorial work is done in-house by the publisher, and the manuscript is sent out for helpful comments by various individuals. The mansucript may go through several drafts. We can envision a similar type of process for computer-based learning materials. However, such a process has seldom been carried out with computer material. It is not even clear when the process should take place. Some editorial work could happen before the material is actually running, while other aspects probably would best wait until after the material is inspectable in computer form. More experience is needed.

The important role of the graphic designer, formatting the screen material, has been suggested. In our work this activity is done directly at the screen, with the graphic designer creating objects, moving them around, changing size and orientation, and effectively 'pasting them down'. An object in this sense might represent pictorial or text information of any complexity or some combination of these. The location of some objects will only be determinable when the dialog is run by the student; the position may be dependent on the progress of the student before this point. Related is the question of when objects vanish from the screen, and the questions of timing between components. As suggested, authors may specify some of these details, but a competent graphic designer with intuition and empirical knowledge about how design affects student usage can play an important role in producing the best materials. Again, a training process is required to acquaint the designer with media capabilities.

One additional type of training is probably needed by the designer. The designer should have some comprehension of the problems of *reading* and how the display mechanism can aid these. The designer should also understand the tradeoffs involved in screen design that are *different* from the tradeoffs in, say, the design of an ad for a magazine. Most important is that blank space in this medium is *free*. Hence, it can be used much more openly as a learning aid. Relatively little material on the screen can emphasize that material, aiding readability.

These design capabilities are not, alas, independent of the details of the display. In our older work with Tektronix displays, we did not have selective erase capability. But in our newer work with stand-alone systems, such capabilities are available. Different design considerations come into effect in these two cases. Even such factors as the number of characters per line and the number of lines that can fit on the screen are important to take into account. We can also do limited animation with the stand-alone system. We believe that these issues and suitable software to handle them are perhaps the most important present transportability problems.

Our older design software is written in APL on the Honeywell Sigma 7. The designer can create objects, move them around the screen, modify their size. The program writes the necessary code, not APL code, for the final program to create the combination chosen by the designer.

The new graphic facilities, using selective erase capabilities and other features not previously available to us, are being developed within the Pascal system developed by Kenneth Bowles at the University of California, San Diego.

One issue is that of who is to enter the *text* in the computer. In the model suggested so far it would appear that the designer would have that task. Yet a designer is not necessarily an excellent typist, and there is much to type. We have given consideration to the issue of how the text can be entered by a competent typist before the designer begins to work.

The task of the programmer is to accept the products of the faculty and the designer and to add the logic decisions necessary for the full working program. As with any programming task, debugging is a major part of this activity. We also insist on readable, well documented programs, realizing that the programs almost certainly will be modified by different programmers. Most of our programming has come from undergraduate students. We have even employed high school students. Our experience has been that the younger the programmers, the more they are likely to fit into our environment. We have also worked with excellent professional programmers.

Our older programming capabilities were a mixture. Much of the analysis of student interaction, and the graphic details, were done in a macro-based system developed at Irvine with a structure not too different from the structure of Tutor, the PLATO language. We used FORTRAN subroutines for calculational aspects, and data base management activities were carried out in COBOL. We avoided calling any of this a 'language,' but regarded it as a collection of facilities to ease the programmer's task.

Our recent activities for stand-alone target machines are within the UCSD Pascal environment, adding procedures to Pascal to ease the programmer's task in connection with such material. Our previous work in the early environment furnishes useful information as to how to proceed in the new environment, but we still have not settled on a particular group of procedures.

One difficulty with most languages is with the input/output routines. They do not provide the flexibility that we need for computer-based learning activities. Furthermore the problems of transportability related to screen design mentioned above interact with the input/output capabilities. Hence, in our newer work with Pascal, we have developed a new set of facilities for input/output and are not using any of the standard Pascal facilities.

PHYSICS EDUCATION, COMPUTERS AND THE FUTURE

Any consideration of the use of the computer with physics classes must, if it is to be realistic, look at the future. The computer will over the next twenty-five years become the major delivery system for learning physics in the United States and all over the world. This does not imply that other learning modes will not continue to exist, but rather that the computer will be the most important. It will largely replace lectures and may even replace textbooks. Although my remarks are particularly directed toward physics, many of the comments have a wider applicability.

The next decade will be a period of turmoil in American education. Projections indicate that 15–20% fewer eighteen year olds will exist, and that the percentage of students who go to universities will decline. Much of this projection is based on hard data. Observers agree that the student population will shift from our traditional student group to one that includes more minority students, older students, and other students with nonstandard backgrounds. Changing student population implies that courses must become more flexible, more able to cope with different backgrounds. Coupled with these developments is increasing public unrest with higher education, unrest often reflected in funding problems for universities. During depressions these problems are likely to be more crippling.

When we examine the future prospects of computers, the situation is much more positive. Computer technology is still in its infancy; costs are declining and capabilities are increasing. While graphics was at one time an expensive addition, now it is available in almost all the cheapest personal computers intended for the home market. Disc technology has moved rapidly with the development of the inexpensive floppy disc. Even more impressive, hard discs of similar structure but with increasing storage are becoming available. The cost of chips comes down steadily, about 25% per year. The new generation of 16-bit microcomputers is only one example of progress in this area.

Of particular interest with computers is the increasing importance of the personal computer, especially in environments where one has not seen computers before. Already approximately 300,000 computers of this type have been sold, mostly to the home market, and projections for the future are many times larger. Because of the nature of the personal computer market, developments are occurring which would have seemed unlikely a few years back. Thus most of the newer home systems offer not only graphic capability but also color.

One of the important features of the personal computer consideration is that it gives an entirely new perspective on what was a perplexing issue of transferability of computer-based learning modules. At the time when everyone was likely to be operating on large-scale timesharing systems, the only way transportability could be achieved was by having the materials available on many different systems. This often led to considerable restrictions in the pedagogical effectiveness of the material. The inexpensive, personal computer gives an entirely different possibility. Since the hardware is inexpensive and since a number of devices will be needed to support a particular course, the hardware will often be purchased precisely *because* the course is available on that particular machine. Thus, the necessity of having everything run on every machine will no longer be necessary. It should also be noted that some of the software systems being developed for personal computers, such as the UCSD

Pascal system, are designed purposely for transportability across a number of systems, another way of easing transportability problems.

The factors discussed in this paper, the effectiveness of the computer as a learning device in many situations, the problems education faces in the next few years and the need for new approaches, and the decreasing cost and increasing capabilities of computers, will combine to assure that the computer will be widely used in physics teaching. It is possible that many beginning courses will be given entirely in this fashion, perhaps in some cases with little resident faculty available at the particular institution.

We can expect a variety of computer-based learning modules to be available, competing materials so that the user will have a choice. Since the computer materials will be developed in an inherently modular form, teachers will also have more freedom than they have at the present time where textbooks determine so many features of the course.

The role of the teacher will change in this process. First, the necessity for preparing sizable amounts of material will mean that many teachers will move from the classroom environment to the developmental environment. The experience of the good teacher is essential in the authoring system. We can expect the learning materials to be more effective than any currently available materials, as our skills increase in producing these materials. This must depend on the input of the best teachers in the country. We can expect that the teachers who do continue with courses will spend more of their time in dealing with students who are either far ahead of the rest of the class or in need of special attention, the kind of attention that can only be given by a dedicated human. These instructors will be less involved in the major delivery mechanisms for learning.

Will the future be better or will students be more poorly served than at present? The decision, at least partially, depends on the present generation of physics teachers.

Comput. & Educ., Vol. 4, pp. 59 to 66
Pergamon Press Ltd 1980. Printed in Great Britain

AN ELECTRONICS COURSE USING AN INTELLIGENT VIDEO FORMAT A PROGRESS REPORT*

KENNETH W. WOOD, WILLIAM D. OHLSEN, HAVEN E. BERGESON
and GRANT W. MASON

University of Utah and Brigham Young University

INTRODUCTION

Some years ago Alfred Bork coined the name 'Intelligent Videodisc' to describe a system of computer-aided instruction (CAI) which incorporates a videodisc player and which, under computer control, can access any materials on the disc which are needed in an instructional program. One side of a videodisc can hold one-half hour of video material, 54,000 still frames, or some combination of the two. The access time for random materials on the disc is only a few seconds. In large quantities, replication of videodiscs is inexpensive. There is also future promise of digital storage of some 30,000 million bits per disc side. (While the storage of video information on the disc is fundamentally partly digital, segments some tens of bits long are occasionally dropped in the recording, making storage of digital information marginal at present.)

It is also possible to use computer-controlled videotape in a CAI system, although random access is much slower, and still frames, while possible, produce tape wear. Nevertheless, the use of videotape will probably be an essential element of any CAI program involving videodisc. Videotape can be edited and changed, while, for the foreseeable future, the content of a videodisc is unchangeable once it has been stamped into the plastic disc. In fact, the most convenient way to produce a videodisc is to make the master from a videotape. Thus a procedure for producing videodiscs is to put the video materials on videotape, test the complete instructional program, modify it, and then commit the video to disc.

In this article, we will modify Bork's term 'Intelligent Videodisc' to 'Intelligent Video Learning' (IVL); this term will refer to any CAI system in which either videotape or videodisc is a part. We will be describing a large effort to develop Intelligent Video Learning courses at the University of Utah and illustrating the program with a particular course, an introduction to electronics for scientists.

THE UTAH PROGRAM FOR INTELLIGENT VIDEO

Organization

An extensive organization for the support of intelligent video course production has been set up at the University of Utah (initially under the direction of the Department of Physics). The project now has five major areas of emphasis: software development, hardware development, authoring, production, and study of intelligent video education. The table below indicates the number of people involved in each of these areas.

	Software	Hardware	Authoring	Production	Education
Full Time	4	0	1	2	1
Part Time	5	2	5	0	2

The software group is concerned with the development of courseware production software to support the authors, to make it easy for them to follow whatever pedagogical goals and techniques they prefer, and to save them time.

Having developed the interface between the computer and the videotape player, the hardware group is now working on an interface between the computer and the videodisc unit†.

The authoring group consists of individuals or teams developing specific courses or tutorials for certain courses. The authors of this article are the authors for the electronics course. We wholeheartedly endorse a suggestion made to us by Alfred Bork that a team is more likely to produce effective

* Development of the course described here is supported by National Science Foundation grant SER-7806412. Transfer to the videodisc and testing of the videodisc format is supported under National Science Foundation grant SED-7900788.

† *Note added in Proof.* An interface to an MCA videodisc unit has now been successfully completed.

interactive materials than is an individual. We share his belief that among the characteristics of high-quality CAI, one of the most important is that it must interact with the student frequently and flexibly.

The production group, a new resource for our authors, helps in entering lessons on the computer, arranging TV studio time, communicating with the software group, improving the displays, etc.

The physics education group consists of graduate students who, for their thesis research, study the effects of various modes of presentation, compare intelligent video instruction with more conventional methods, study the learning process as it relates to physics at the university level, and develop improvements in the teaching of physics.

Hardware

Along with a number of other groups interested in CAI, we have decided to use small stand-alone computers for course creation as well as for course delivery. At present the Terak 8510/A microcomputer system is used for both. This LSI-11† based system has 56 kbytes of memory, an eight inch floppy-disc drive, and a black and white monitor with 240×320 dot-matrix graphics. The text display is 24 lines of 80 characters, and it is completely independent of the graphics. Thus, text and graphics can be displayed simultaneously anywhere on the screen. In addition, the character set is software definable. This software defined character set can be edited to create special symbols for an IVL lesson. The educational users price of $5500 for the Terak is rather high for student use, but a satisfactory lower priced delivery system with similar features is anticipated in the near future.

In the current configuration the video from the videotape player is presented on a separate nine-inch Sony color TV set. The videotape unit is a Sony VP2000 player. These two units add about $1700 to the cost of the delivery system. In addition the system uses a TV controller which occupies the last LSI-11 circuit board slot in the Terak and a TV-player interface located external to the computer near the TV player. Both of the latter units have been designed and constructed in-house. Care has been taken to separate the functions of the various circuit boards in such a manner that a change in computer type or video player type results in a minimum number of circuit boards which need to be changed. The controller-interface unit adds about $1500 to the system cost (though commercial production would reduce the cost significantly).

From the software point of view, the controller is a seven register device (four 16-bit data registers, a control and status register, a 16-bit count register, and an 8-bit pause register) with interrupt generation capabilities. The unit utilizes the videotape SMPTE time code to locate and play a selected video portion when so instructed by the lesson program. Any given frame can be located and used as the start or stop frame of a TV segment. The unit can also provide a 'tear-free' freeze frame presentation, but due to tape wear, this capability is really only useful for preparing authors for the improved performance of the videodisc.

Facilities

The University of Utah administration has been very helpful in launching this program. They are now in the process of providing a separate building in which the software development, authoring, and courseware development can take place. It should provide a comfortable setting in which authors from other institutions can spend a sabbatical leave creating courseware. (Interested potential authors are invited to inquire.)

Utah authoring system

Richard C. Brandt and a number of associates from the University of Utah have developed an efficient authoring system to permit authors unskilled in programming to create IVL lessons. (This development occurred after consultation with Alfred Bork and others from the University of California at Irvine and with a group from the University of California at San Diego led by Kenneth Bowles.)

The Utah Authoring System forms a common data-base structure for all IVL lessons. The data base consists of a file of all the text for a lesson, a file of all the graphics for the lesson, and a file of instructions that, along with the student answer, determines the lesson flow. For example, the instruction file would have commands that could cause any of the following to occur: display text, display graphics, display a combination of text and graphics, run a particular segment of videotape (with sound alone, picture alone or both together), act on a student answer (read in the answer, compare it to a list of anticipated answers, and branch based on the results of that comparison), or initiate an independently-authored "special" program.

† LSI-11 is a copyrighted product of the Digital Equipment Corporation.

The authoring system is based on the University of California at San Diego (UCSD) version of the PASCAL programming language. This choice was made both because of the elegance and power of PASCAL and because its use promotes portability of software and courseware between various computers. It does require, however, that any user have UCSD PASCAL™ available. The growing popularity and easy availability of UCSD PASCAL™ suggests that this limitation is not serious.

To an author, the system consists of a number of packages which aid him in creation, modification, and assembling of text, graphics, and animation materials. It also contains packages to help him assemble these materials into lessons with great depth of branching capabilities, flexible response to student answers, ability to find video segments and to start or stop a tape or disc player, and capability to run student-controlled simulations. Another program (the interpreter) runs the actual lessons. Physicists, engineers, and chemists will appreciate the capability in the interpreter to compare inputs in algebraic form with the author's algebraic answer to see if they are equivalent. (The two forms are compared using the rules of algebra.) Finally, there are packages to permit an author or, even more importantly, a user to make modifications in a completed lesson with relative ease. Further details can be found in the appendix to this article.

Courses under production

Three courseware development efforts are now in progress. One involves tutorial segments for elementary physics for non-technical majors. Many of the tutorials are in rough but complete form and have been used successfully for the past year; they are now being polished by our production group and are in use in two courses. A nearly complete stand-alone, one-quarter course in electronics is now being used and tested. A complete introductory physics course for non-technical majors is in preparation, and is planned for use during Autumn quarter of 1980.

THE IVL COURSE IN MODERN ELECTRONICS

The most difficult and important parts in the creation of any IVL (or CAI) course are the formation of the overall concepts of the course and the pedagogical design of individual lessons. The overall concept and some of the aspects of individual lesson design are strongly influenced by the nature of a popular course in electronics given at the University of Utah since 1970[1,2]. However, the use of IVL opens up so many new possibilities that each lesson requires an extended conference between authors to determine the teaching strategy and the tools to be used. Nevertheless, no attempt is made to create a virtuoso IVL course; uniquely IVL approaches are used only when they seem to provide the best opportunity for student learning. We will now describe several major pedagogical and content features and how they are implemented.

1. *The course is highly individualized*

The course provides many routes through the material. Reviews and special helps occur frequently. At various points in the lessons, a student can ask to see a menu and can choose to re-enter the lesson at a variety of points listed on it. A student who already understands the material in question finds that he can proceed through the lesson rapidly, while a student who has difficulty finds that a great deal of prompting is given.

2. *The course emphasizes use of high-performance integrated circuits*

The sophistication of modern integrated circuits is such that the student can often concentrate on the function of an active element in his circuit without the frustration of dealing with an endless number of problems related to such things as biasing, input impedance, offset voltages and currents, etc. These matters can be introduced after the student has built simple, successful circuits.

The rapid evolution of semiconductor devices presents the same problem to IVL that it does to a textbook writer: the particular devices used in the expository part of the course may be obsolete one or two years later, with the result that it may be desirable to use different ones in the current laboratory. This difficulty might be regarded as a strength for the student in that he faces the same problem in completing the course that he must deal with subsequently in his professional career. The real goal must be to teach students to work from specification sheets of popular devices rather than to limit them to those covered in the original exposition.

3. *The course emphasizes breadth over depth*

This course is meant to service scientists and others for whom electronics is a tool rather than an end in itself. Such users are rarely interested in optimizing circuit performance or in marginal cost reduction. What they really need is quick solutions to electronics problems so that they can proceed with other more pressing problems. Hence, they need to be exposed to a large number of types of circuits which can be implemented easily. It should be noted that modern function-oriented integrated circuits are so simple to use that students can learn to design, test, and debug manifestly useful circuits beginning with the second lesson of the course.

4. *The course emphasizes circuit design rather than circuit analysis*

The traditional approach emphasizes circuit analysis which of necessity uses detailed circuit models. Such an approach is fine if one has a circuit and wishes to optimize its performance. In systematic ways one can determine the effects of changes in various circuit parameters until excellent performance is achieved. Such an approach is excellent for an engineer who can spend a great amount of time on a circuit which will then be reproduced many times. However, it is a poor approach for a physicist who may wish only to quickly build one working interface between two commercial circuits. It is far more appropriate for him to design from very simple circuit models and then to treat features left out of those models as perturbations which might require circuit modification. He should also use higher performance integrated circuits than may be absolutely necessary if doing so will save him time in implementing the circuit.

Circuit design is a rather difficult process to teach in a traditional lecture setting. Many students are still naive enough to expect unique correct answers to given problems. Yet many different circuit designs can all satisfy the requirement that a circuit perform within certain limits. IVL facilitates the step-by-step design process by allowing the student to know when a given decision is acceptable; he can then proceed with confidence to the next step.

5. *The course is strongly laboratory oriented*

In earlier version of the course there was a 2-h laboratory session for each lecture period. A similar balance occurs in the IVL course, but of course, the lessons are not restricted to the usual 50-min lecture. A typical laboratory assignment is to design, test, and debug a circuit which performs within certain specified limits. No credit is given for performance outside the limits, and full credit is given for performance inside the limits. Furthermore, 60% of the course grade is determined by the laboratory work.

Each student is provided with a breadboard which contains three power supplies, a three-frequency clock generator, four light-emitting diode logic indicators, four data switches, and two non-bouncing logic switches. (These switches and indicators are designed to produce or indicate the presence of either a logic '1' or '0' for integrated circuits in either the transistor-transistor logic (TTL) family or the complementary metal-oxide-surface (CMOS) family when operating between ground and $+5$ V.) There is also a solderless system for connecting components.

The type of laboratory required in the course can be given without any use of IVL. However, IVL does make it much easier. First of all, instruction on the use of breadboards, oscilloscopes, multimeters, and the like can be done effectively using video materials (see Fig. 1). (This is one place where laboratory-assistant time can be saved.) Secondly, in a traditional laboratory, an assignment must often use several new concepts; as a result, the student may not be able to disentangle problems associated with different concepts. Computer simulations can greatly reduce the problem by involving the student with one new concept at a time. Thus he needn't passively absorb several new ideas before he can work with a circuit. For example, it is natural to bridge the gap between linear circuits and digital circuits by introducing voltage comparators and Schmitt triggers, both normally in a single lesson. A simulated laboratory design of a voltage comparator (see Fig. 2) can fix the idea of an output having only two states before the student must meet the complications of dealing with positive feedback and hysteresis. In the traditional format, it is likely that both would be dealt with in a single lecture, leaving the student no opportunity to examine carefully the simpler comparator before having to consider the more complex Schmitt trigger.

6. *The course content revolves around useful circuits*

The first lesson reviews Ohm's Law, and presents applications with series and parallel resistor circuits, voltage dividers, input and output resistances, impedance matching and mismatching, and power transfer. From then on the approach is to couple tightly electronic principles and their practical uses rather than covering the principles of electronic circuits first and then considering applications. For example, the second lesson teaches negative feedback in connection with inverting and non-inverting operational amplifier circuits. Similarly, the fourth lesson teaches positive feedback

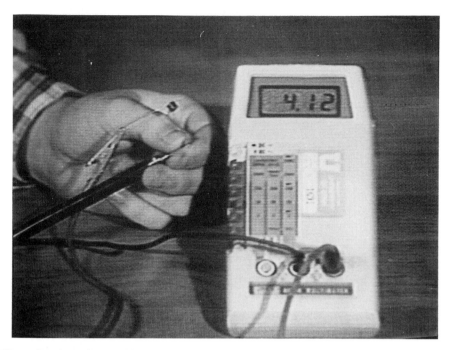

Fig. 1. One frame from a video segment demonstrating use of a digital multimeter to measure the resistance of thermistor. The resistance is measured at room temperature and again when warmed by a human hand. (This segment is part of a lesson on Schmitt triggers, in which an alarm is to be made to sound when the thermistor is warm and is to be turned off when the thermistor returns to room temperature.)

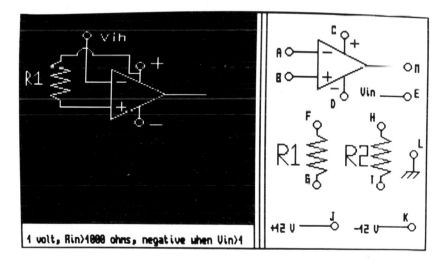

Fig. 2. Partially completed laboratory simulation. The black-on-white portion of the display at the right provides set of components from which the student is to construct a voltage comparator circuit with a specified threshold. The circuit is assembled in the white-on-black portion of the display at the left under the student's direction. When the circuit is completed correctly, the student is asked to specify component values. If the student commands a disastrous connection (e.g. connect +12 V to −12 V) a descending audio siren is heard, and the circuit is destroyed; after an explanation, the circuit is restored without the fatal connection, and the student is allowed to proceed.

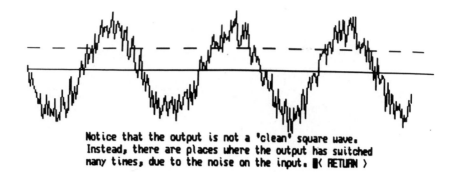

Notice that the output is not a 'clean' square wave.
Instead, there are places where the output has switched
many times, due to the noise on the input. < RETURN >

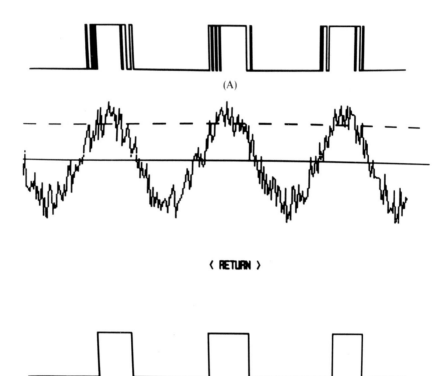

(A)

< RETURN >

(B)

Fig. 3. Student-controlled simulation of the response of a voltage comparator and of a Schmitt trigger to a noisy signal. The student can specify the signal level, the noise levels, and the 'trip points' of the comparator and of the Schmitt trigger. In Fig. 3(A), the upper part of the figure shows a noisy sine wave; the solid line represent the ground level while the dashed line represents the comparison input voltage to a voltage comparator. The bottom part of the figure shows the output of the voltage comparator; the rapid switching of the output as the signal crosses the comparison voltage clearly shows the effect of noise. In Fig. 3(B), a noisy signal with the same parameters as that of Fig. 3(A) is shown. Here, the dashed line represents the 'trip point' of a Schmitt trigger. The clean switching at the output of a properly-designed Schmitt trigger is demonstrated at the bottom of Fig. 3(B). All signals are drawn in real time on the screen. The Schmitt trigger 'trip point' changes with each change of output.

in connection with the Schmitt trigger. In the sixth lesson Boolean algebra is taught in connection with the use of logic circuits involved in solutions to specific examples of problems. (In such lessons the student must generalize the applications of the principles learned as he designs circuits for the laboratory assignments. The IVL version gives additional opportunities for student use of the principles as they are learned.)

7. The course covers a wide variety of linear and digital circuits

After the Ohm's Law applications, the course covers negative-feedback circuits using operational amplifiers. Performance is first derived taking the limit of infinite open-loop gain for operational amplifiers; then students are introduced to the equivalent concept that, if the output isn't saturated, the inverting input voltage must be 'virtually equal' to the non-inverting input voltage. This powerful concept allows the student to calculate almost trivially the behaviour of amplifiers, adders, integrators, differentiators, difference amplifiers, and elementary analog computer circuits. Input-offset voltages and currents are introduced as perturbations whose effects must either be shown to be negligible or corrected for.

The use of saturated output circuits bridges the gap between analog and digital circuits. The use of voltage comparators introduces the concept of two-state outputs, and the use of Schmitt triggers introduces the concept of hysteresis (see Fig. 3).

Simple logic circuits are shown as solutions to a number of practical problems ('three-way light switch', 'safety controls', etc.). Then counting circuits, digital decoding, and digital displays are covered. CMOS circuits are used for the actual hardware implementation.

RC circuits and exponential charging and discharging are applied to one-shot multivibrators, square-wave oscillators, and timing circuits.

Complex impedances are introduced and derived in conjunction with filtering circuits including active filters.

The applications of diodes is made clear in their uses in rectifying, clipping, clamping, and voltage doubling circuits. The transistor finds its first application as a switch in a sawtooth waveform generator and subsequently in a voltage-controlled amplifier. Transistors are then used to increase the current-handling capacity of operational amplifier circuits.

8. The IVL course provides opportunities for discovery learning

One example involves computer-simulated dynamic display of wave forms. Students are allowed to vary the parameters in an RC circuit with a stepfunction input before seeing the differential equation describing the circuit behaviour. The behaviour of the circuit then becomes a physical effect to him before it becomes a formal solution to a differential equation. The expected consequence is that passive integrators or differentiators will be thought of naturally as tools for wave shaping.

A second example of the use of IVL involves the truth tables for logic circuits. At times they are simply provided and the student is required to deduce various effects. At other times, however, the student is required to vary the different inputs of a graphically-simulated integrated logic circuit, observe the output, and fill in the truth table.

9. The IVL course includes automatic record keeping

A record is kept of the branching that occurs for each student as he progresses through the IVL lessons. Two benefits arise from the recording of individual student tracks through the IVL materials. First, students having exceptional difficulty are identified for special help. Second, the course itself is evaluated in part by keeping track of average student time spent, the number of correct responses, and the number of incorrect responses to each question. Questions requiring an inordinate amount of time and/or having few correct responses can be revised, or the preceding explanatory material can be improved. Additional evaluation occurs as students are invited to leave anonymous comments at the end of each lesson. These comments are entered by the student via the keyboard and are stored on the floppy disc which also serves as the source of the lesson he has been using.

Records are also kept of test performance for possible grading purposes. However, the course is rather strongly oriented toward mastery learning, so that it isn't clear just what meaning is to be attached to course grades.

Status

Most of the course has now been taught as a free-standing IVL course without lectures. Student response has been favorable. The laboratory simulations have been received especially well. In them, students assemble circuits on the graphics screen and then specify component values. They are then told whether the circuit responds within specifications.

The most significant evaluation of this material will occur when students are paid to participate in tests. Some students will be exposed to segments of the subject taught with the more traditional approach while the rest will be taught the same subjects with IVL. Not only will their subsequent success or lack thereof in the laboratory be compared, but the average time required for them to master the subject will be compared. Then we will have a much better idea of the value of IVL in a course with a strong laboratory orientation.

Acknowledgements—A special expression of gratitude must be given to Richard Brandt who saw very early that the most precious resource to be conserved in courseware production is the time of the authors. He then supervised a group of programmers who created an efficient authoring system. He also developed the hardware for the video interfaces and controllers. Association with John DeFord and Robert Kadesch who are working on other IVL courses has been stimulating and most helpful. Finally, as with many others, we are pleased to acknowledge both the pioneering CAI achievements of Alfred Bork and his constant encouragement that we put the student at the center of any teaching materials we create.

REFERENCES

1. Bergeson H. E., An electronics course emphasizing circuit design, *Am. J. Phys.* **43**, 223 (1975).
2. Bergeson H. E. and Cassiday G. L., On the teaching of electronics to scientists, *Adv. Electron. Electron Phys.* **45**, 253 (1978).

APPENDIX—DETAILS OF THE UTAH AUTHORING SYSTEM

The authoring package consists of the following sub-packages:

TEXTEDIT permits the user to create and edit textpage files. A textpage file is an array of characters displayed on the screen during an actual lesson.
GRAFEDIT permits the user to edit and create graphics for lessons.
ANIMATE provides the user with a tool for creating simple animations for lessons.
BUILDER permits the user to construct complicated lessons without programming.
LINKER provides the capability to link lesson segments into a large lesson.
INTERP is the program that actually runs the lesson. In addition it outputs files on student performance.
DISASSEM and ASSEMBL provide the user with a tool to make simple lesson modifications and to update old instruction files.
LESEVAL provides some course management and lesson evaluation capabilities.

UTILITY PROGRAMS:
GRAFPROCS converts graphics files to a format (picture files) usable in lessons.
PLOTTER permits drawing of picture files on a HIPLOT plotter.
SEQDATGEN provides information to INTERP.
VIDEOSEL selects videotape sections.
DOCUM provides formatted output to either a DECwriter or a Diablo printer.

All of these programs are designed for ease of use. Every program has a 'promptline' which lists the commands available. After typing the capitalized letter designating the desired command, a new promptline appears containing additional commands and information. For example, the main promptline for GRAFEDIT is:

GRAFEDIT: Clear Display Hairs File Objects Set Pages Quit

A user who typed 'O' for 'objects' will then see a new promptline:

GRAFEDIT OBJECTS: Arc Bez Circle Fill Line User-defined Quit

He could then type 'C' for circle; he then would see the next promptline:

GRAFEDIT Circle: Add Delete Replace Quit

The user can add circles to the picture by typing 'A', delete them by typing 'D', or change them (i.e. replace one circle with a different one) by typing 'R'. If Add is chosen, the promptline displayed is:

CIRCLE ADD Curser: ⟨arrows⟩ '.' ⟨etx⟩ accepts ⟨esc⟩ rejects

This promptline provides the user with the following information: the cursor can be positioned using the directional arrows on the keyboard; the center of the circle is determined by placing the cursor at the appropriate position and then typing a dot (via the 'period' key) and the radius is then determined by placing the cursor somewhere on the circumference and again typing a dot (as soon as the two dots are typed, the circle is drawn automatically); typing the key labeled 'etx' causes the circles drawn to be accepted as part of the graphics picture being drawn; typing the key labeled 'esc' will cause rejection of the circles just completed.

After typing the 'esc' or 'etx' key, the system goes back to the Circle prompt line, where the author is prompted to Add, Delete, Replace, or Quit. If 'Q' is typed, the system goes back further to the Objects prompt. Here the user can choose any of the available objects ('L' for ability to draw lines, 'U' to call for objects previously defined by the user, etc.) or he can type 'Q' to quit. Typing 'Q' would bring him back to the main promptline for the GRAFEDIT editor.

Comput. & Educ., Vol. 4, pp. 67 to 75
Pergamon Press Ltd 1980. Printed in Great Britain

COMPUTATION AS A PHYSICAL AND INTELLECTUAL ENVIRONMENT FOR LEARNING PHYSICS

A. A. diSessa

Massachusetts Institute of Technology

INTRODUCTION

This paper attempts to convey some of the flavor and scope of an approach to using computers in education developed over the last ten years mainly at the Logo Laboratory, a joint endeavor of M.I.T.'s Artificial Intelligence Laboratory and Division for Study and Research in Education. Although our strongest suit has been mathematics, the past four or five years has seen increasing concern with physics, the topic here.

It is not an easy matter to give a concise description of a rather large scaled and long term research and development project, especially in education. The easiest route is to give a synopsis of students taught, courses given, equipment and languages used, etc. I shall do some of that. However, what is more important is the complex texture of values, goals, heuristics and central ideas which guide the project and are mutually influenced through its course*.

In order to bring out some of that detail, I have chosen to deal with only two main topics, each in some depth. The topics are in fact one of our earliest products, a computational treatment of orbital mechanics, and one of our most recent, a computer environment for teaching Newton's Laws. In addition to giving some sense of history, these happen to be emblematic of two important principles guiding our work generally. Before turning to them, I will introduce our project and central character, the turtle, for those not familiar with them.

Turtle graphics and the Logo language

Imagine a creature, either a small robot or a cursor on a display screen, which responds to commands typed at a computer terminal. FORWARD 100 causes the turtle to move 100 units in the direction he is facing. RIGHT 90 or LEFT 45 cause him to turn in place to the right or left the specified number of degrees. Figure 1 shows a sample of the sort of things a turtle is capable of producing.

The turtle was invented as part of a computer language called Logo which was explicitly designed for children. Despite its simplicity at entrance, the language contains extremely powerful constructs, e.g. recursion and full list processing capability, which mean no upper limit to the kind of project students can tackle, regardless of age. We regularly use the same system for students at the third grade level (making drawings like Fig. 1), high school (studying the mathematical properties of those same sorts of figures[1]), and M.I.T. undergraduates (simulating and studying geometry on curved surfaces and even in Einstein's curved space-time[2]).

Turtle geometry

Evidently the turtle's domain is geometry, but a geometry of a very different character than textbook Euclidean geometry.

1. It is based on anthropomorphism more than formalism. Of course, turtle geometry does have a rich formal structure which could be based on axioms and the like, but what is more important, the initial elements are not abstractions, but simple images which the student can model quite well from his own experience. This is an example of the first of our two principles—developing mathematics and sciences which are based on the learner's world as much as on the mathematician's or scientist's.

2. Turtle geometry is process oriented and constructive, a fact which pays dividends in several ways. First, the environment in which it is embedded, turtle graphics and a programming language, is also process oriented. This makes for an important synergy between the mathematics and the computer environment. For example, concepts useful in turtle geometry are much the same as those needed to discuss any process: Awareness of such concepts as *state* (the turtle's state has two parts,

---

* In a deep sense, Logo's 'philosophy' is one of its most important products. A more complete view can be found in Ref. [8].

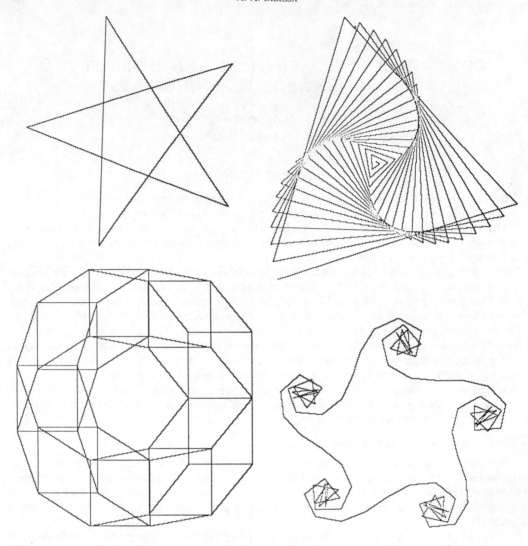

Fig. 1. Some figures drawn by a turtle. (These are at most four line programs.)

position and heading) and of available *state change operators* (FORWARD and the turn commands) comes early, a not insignificant fact for those interested in teaching physics.

Second, the process orientation gives synthesis an important role, allowing students to become initiators and explorers far more than with subjects like Euclidean geometry. Returning agency to students is a high priority at the Logo project. We rely heavily on elementary school students' constructive knowledge and already established aesthetic in pictures and drawing to allow *them* to propose projects and studies—not just wait for the next exercise.

It should be evident that the above advantages rely heavily on the existence of the turtle graphics/Logo environment. This is in fact the second of our major principles, constructing computational environments which embody the domain content and allow students free, play-like access to it.

The final advantage of a process geometry which is especially important to the transition we are about to make, to physics, is that it is a local and differential method. It is a vital characteristic of the laws of nature that they are both local and differential. It is as well embarrassing pedagogically that students traditionally have to wait so long to meet anything remotely similar in their schooling.

A turtle geometry theorem

Before turning to physics a concrete example is presented of the above characteristics: the turtle geometric description of a circle.

FORWARD ⟨any small distance⟩
RIGHT ⟨any small angle⟩
REPEAT

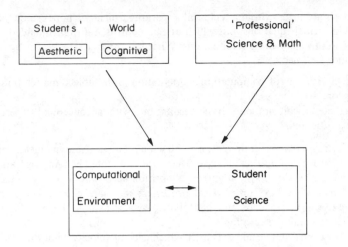

Fig. 2. Schematic of the development of a learning environment.

Notice the description is local, differential and constructive. It is a good 'first differential equation' to introduce students to those ideas. The anthropomorphic, non-formal nature of turtle geometry allows elementary school students to understand that description, even suggest it themselves. It plays a role in turtle geometry and turtle physics akin to the role of the simple harmonic oscillator in physics; a simple, thoroughly understood process which seems ubiquitous as an element of analysis in more complicated situations†.

One technical fact about that description of a circle is relevant for later discussion. The ratio ⟨distance⟩/⟨angle⟩ is proportional to (equal to, if angle is in radians) the radius of the circle. That's a simple theoretical result for high school students and an empirical result routinely discovered by elementary school students in trying to draw circles of different sizes.

Summarized in Fig. 2 is the sort of development which the Logo Project is attempting. We draw on two sources: the structure of science and mathematics as given us by scientists and mathematicians; the realities of the student's mental world including what we know of naive knowledge state and 'information processing capabilities', but equally of student's aesthetic sensibilities. What we produce is a synergistic pair consisting of a computational environment (turtle graphics and Logo) and a student science (turtle geometry). The synergy is two way: The computational environment is designed to embody the fundamental structures we want students to learn; we infuse the science with a computational orientation where appropriate to help unify the students' experience and take advantage of the fact that 'process knowledge' is an essential part of many sciences, particularly in physics.

RECONCEPTUALIZING ORBITAL MECHANICS

Euclidean geometry was a wonderful achievement. But in the form in which it appears in text books, it was motivated by a search for certainty, elegance and conciseness far beyond what those who first proposed the ideas needed. They merely wanted to measure their fields. Students, like the first geometers, have little aesthetic for such elegance or certainty. A task of more interest to them, and one they already know a good deal about, is drawing interesting pictures and patterns and understanding the result. That is why turtle geometry was invented.

Principle One
The science of scientists is for scientists. Let's invent new sciences for students.

Orbital mechanics is a topic which might really interest students. Navigating a spaceship is quite an attractive task. Consider the popularity of the computer game Spacewar. Understanding and exploring the rich gravitational phenomena of the Solar System and galaxy seems quite motivating. Unfortunately, traditional approaches are lacking. Early treatments (junior high school and even most high school courses) are content with dispensing results; orbits are ellipses with focus at the sun, etc. Later treatments are content with justifying those results with derivations. But these are hardly the kind of results students can use in navigating spaceships or studying natural perturbations of orbits. More-

† It turns out, for example, that any turtle program which repeats something over and over, no matter how complicated the repeated thing, can be modeled by a uniform circular motion. See Ref. [2].

over, the derivations are made within a technical apparatus which (we hope) students will eventually master, namely differential equations, but which at this point is not even intended to give students tools for generalizing to more complex situations. What follows is a sketch of a treatment of orbital mechanics[3] which is aimed at:

1. Continuing the synergy of computational orientation with subject matter (indeed, continuing based on turtle geometry).

2. Providing students with not only basic results, but with a conceptual repertoire extendable beyond those results as well.

We start with a computational formulation of Newton's Laws. The dynamical state of a physical object is given by its position and its velocity. There are two state changing operations. The first is internal and automatic; *velocity* constantly updates position according to $\mathbf{x} \leftarrow \mathbf{x} + \mathbf{v}\Delta t$. The second is the only external handle we have on physical processes; the state change operator *force* controls velocity according to $\mathbf{v} \leftarrow \mathbf{v} + (\mathbf{F}/m)\Delta t$. In what follows, we also assume the 'equal area in equal time' form of angular momentum conservation.

Because the only external state changer is force which acts on velocity—not directly on position—it is almost always appropriate to look at dynamical situations in velocity space. That is the key heuristic which we will apply. Note that within the computational system represented by our two updating equations, velocity space is no more abstract than is ordinary position space. In a computer program one could just as easily display v as x.

The first result we aim for is a qualitative one: orbits close. In particular we will show that an orbit like Fig. 3 is impossible. Applying our key heuristic, we look to velocity space.

If an orbit closes and repeats itself, certainly the velocity space path must close. Is closure in velocity space sufficient to ensure position space closure? Indeed so, for if velocity returned to its initial value while position did not, equal area would no longer be swept out in equal time. (Nor would energy be conserved.)

The problem is reduced to showing that all the kicks (changes in velocity), $(\mathbf{F}/m)\Delta t$, sum to zero. Looking for a plausible mechanism for kick cancellation, we focus attention on segments of the orbit directly opposite, subtending equal angles through the sun. (Equal time and equal length segments are other candidates, but are easily discarded.)

Is $(F/m)\Delta t \propto (1/r^2)\Delta t$ the same for such pieces of orbit? We note that, since those sections of orbit are similar, the area swept out is proportional to dimension squared ($\Delta A = (1/2)r^2\Delta\theta$). This permits us to use the one constant of motion we have assumed, $\Delta A/\Delta t$, as follows:

$$(F/m)\Delta t \propto \Delta t/r^2 \propto \Delta t/\Delta A \propto (\Delta A/\Delta t)^{-1} = \text{constant}$$

Hence we have shown that the magnitude of kicks for opposing segments of orbit are proportional (in the same way) to a constant, hence are the same. Since the kicks point in opposite directions, they cancel pair by pair in summing kicks all the way around the sun.

The short proportionality argument above actually gives us a bit stronger result. It did not depend on kicks being from opposing segments of orbit, merely segments subtending the same angle from the sun. Hence we conclude what we call Kepler's Zeroeth Law:

Gravity provides equal kicks in equal angles.

Any turtle geometer's instincts should be aroused—there must be a circle (of kicks) nearby! Being a bit more careful, we observe that if an orbit is divided into equal angle chunks, the kicks all have equal magnitude. The 're-aiming' from one kick direction to the next (to point toward the sun) is

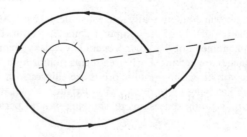

Fig. 3. An impossible orbit.

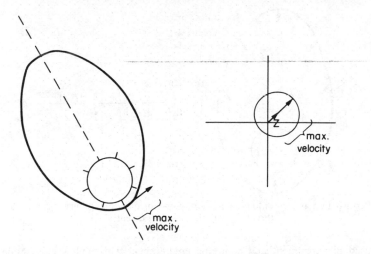

Fig. 4. Maximum velocity is in the direction of displacement of center of velocity space circle.
That direction is perpendicular to the major axis of the orbit.

exactly the angle change in the planet as seen from the sun between chunks, hence the same previously chosen constant. The velocity space path is thus generated by

FORWARD ⟨a constant kick⟩
TURN ⟨a constant angle⟩
REPEAT.

Orbits in velocity space are always circles. Following through with proportionality constants shows
the ratio of kick to angle (by our turtle theorem, this is the radius of the velocity space circle) is k/L
where k is the gravitational force constant, $k = GM$ in conventional terms, and L is angular momentum.

Notice, true to turtle methods, we have discovered a circle by its intrinsic characteristics and by its
process of generation. We do not yet know where the circle is located. The short argument depicted in
Fig. 4 shows that the displacement of the center of the circle (indicated by z) determines the orienta-
tion of the position space orbit which must be elongated perpendicular to z. $|z|$ is in fact proportional
to the eccentricity, a perfectly obvious guess.

What should we expect if a perturbation is applied to the orbit, say a rocket impulse or a force
from a 'solar wind?' Without any detailed analysis, merely realizing that force affects velocity, we
should expect that the velocity space circle should be moved in the direction of the perturbing force.
Thus we have

Perturbation Heuristic: z *moves in the direction of the perturbation force.*

A simple analytic derivation of the way z actually moves shows that this is almost always a good
approximation, and when the radius of the circle (angular momentum) doesn't change, one has the
remarkable result that the change in z is exactly the kick applied by the perturbation force, $(F/m)\Delta t$.
Notice that according to Fig. 4, this has the extremely counter-intuitive result that a perturbation of a
circular orbit causes elongation perpendicular to the direction of the perturbation force.

On a computer display, seeing the z vector can make intricate orbital manoevers of a spaceship, not
trivial, but at least doable and understandable. Systematic perturbations become qualitatively and
sometimes quantitatively understandable. For example, we can quite easily qualitatively duplicate
Dicke and Goldenberg's calculation of the effect of an oblateness of the sun (extra mass near the
equator). By symmetry the perturbation force must be radial, preserving angular momentum and the
radius of the velocity space circle. Again by symmetry (Fig. 5) the perturbation force must average
along the major axis of the orbit. Thus the change in z is perpendicular to z;z rotates; the orbit
precesses.

Complementing this turtle and computation-influenced treatment of orbital mechanics, we enhance
the turtle graphics/Logo environment with an orbital simulation to get students started [4]. The
simulation is written in Logo and meant to be transparent and modular so the student can amend or
expand at will. In particular, provisions are made so that one can trivially run student-written
spaceship controlling (or whatever) programs simultaneously with the basic simulation.

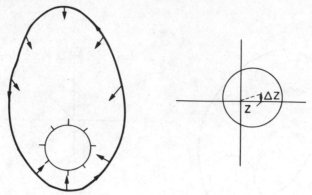

Fig. 5. Perturbation averages along major axis, perpendicular to z. Hence z rotates and so does the orbit, without changing eccentricity.

We have used this treatment and computer environment with high school students and undergraduates over the last three years. Some of our favorite student projects have been a spaceship which under program control intercepts an orbiting target; a spaceship instrument panel designed to aid a pilot 'dock' in orbit; a project studying catastrophic interactions between a pair of orbiting objects, interactions which throw one of them out of orbit; and extending the simulation to three dimensions.

DYNATURTLE: SPONTANEOUS LEARNING IN A COMPUTATIONAL ENVIRONMENT

The preceding example concentrated on the conceptual side of our work. This second example puts the spotlight on the computational environment.

Our project has documented many kinds of mathematical learning which occur *spontaneously* in children working with turtle graphics [5]. Ideas of similarity, modular arithmetic and some of the simple theorems of turtle geometry are examples. (I emphasize students discover the theorem and its usefulness, not its proof.) This kind of learning is immensely attractive. Imagine bypassing the authoritarian classroom, dull texts and lectures, tedious drill and practice exercises, freeing students to be their own intellectual agents, and yet still having them learn fundamental math and physics.

There are good reasons to believe that such learning is not just wishful thinking. As existence proofs consider pre-schoolers learning typically over a thousand words of vocabulary and to produce sentences which follow English's complex grammatical rules, or, for those familiar with Piaget, the remarkable intellectual development demonstrated in his experiments with children. A crucial element seems to be an extended interaction with an environment which functionally embodies the structures to be learned. A family which speaks English is such an environment.

Principle Two
We would like to construct computational environments which embody physics in such a way that students exploring those environments teach themselves the physics.

The orbital section suggests the road we would take in embodying a computational environment—turtles in velocity space. Actually, mostly for technological reasons, what we implemented was a simple hybrid between position and velocity turtles called a dynaturtle.

A dynaturtle reacts to right and left commands in just the way a regular turtle does, but there is no direct position changing command. Instead, one acts on the velocity part of state with a KICK command which provides an impulse in the direction the turtle is facing. If no kick commands are given, the dynaturtle travels with constant velocity in a straight line. Thus the dynaturtle obeys Newton's First and Second Laws (without the effect of mass). In order to effect real time control, we also augmented the computational environment so that students could arrange to have single key strokes instantly execute any sequence of Logo commands or procedures, e.g. K causes KICK 30, R causes RIGHT 30, etc.

The dynaturtle has been tried out with a group of sixth grade students who were nearing the end of a 10 week, 1-h per day exposure to Logo[5]. Briefly, the results were as follows:

1. The students were interested enough to spend a significant proportion of the two weeks during which dynaturtle was available working with it in the games we provided as starters, modifying those games, and engaging in self-chosen projects.

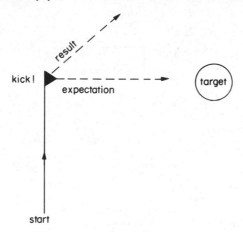

Fig. 6. The Corner Strategy expectation and result.

2. The students' development in understanding dynaturtle followed a pattern characterized by a sequence of proposed strategies (which succeeded or failed) *not* by a continuous acquisition of skill. More than that, the strategies fell into only a few simple classes.

3. The most prominent class of strategies showed a remarkably resilient 'Aristotelian' expectation in the students: that dynaturtle would go in the direction kicked. For example, a frequent strategy for hitting a target at bearing 45° from the dynaturtle was to 'kick up' to move up the screen, then, when the dynaturtle was at the same height as the target, kick toward the target (Fig. 6).

Results 2 and 3 together indicate a rather strong link between the dynaturtle and students' naive conceptual structure as regards mechanics. Looking toward explicitly learning 'proper' Newtonian mechanics, there are two other particularly pedagogically encouraging features of the results: Almost all reacted in essentially the same way to the environment; what they did seemed to involve discrete 'theories' or at least particular strategies and expectations much more than just a gradual increase of skill, which would be of far less value.

To give more substance to the image of pedagogy based on these naive 'theories' an example is presented: a particular element in the students' learning. That element arose in the already mentioned right angle strategy for reaching a target. The method several students spontaneously proposed to debug this (and the rest adopted instantly when it was suggested to them) was dubbed 'antikick' by one of the students whose idea it was. When reaching the height of the target, instead of kicking toward the target, kick opposite the initial kick which started motion, i.e. kick downward. This antikick cancels the starting kick and results in a stopped dynaturtle which can then be aimed to shoot directly at the target.

I am suggesting the antikick idea as an intermediate concept for students long before they can deal with the Newtonian dynamic in its full generality. Note the following:

1. Antikick, while extremely natural and intuitive for students, is conceptually restricted. Students *never* used it in situations other than canceling starting kicks in order to stop, although, of course, Newton allows kick–antikick pairs to be applied to good advantage superimposed on an initial velocity and even with other kicks between, separating the kick–antikick pair.

2. The idea is immediately powerful for the students; it allows them to negotiate almost any path with kick–antikick pairs at opposite ends of path segments.

3. The antikick has no reflection in standard curriculum, a fact symptomatic of why one must conventionally wait so long to introduce students to Newton's Laws.

4. Antikick has a natural conceptual development which can bring students, for example, to a good understanding of the initial situation which it avoided, composing a force with an established velocity in a non-linear configuration, a situation which is extremely problematical for non-physicists of all ages. To see how this development can come about consider a thought experiment which was proposed to one of the students. Think of the antikick and the reaimed kick toward the target as coming very close together in time, essentially simultaneous. Now it is quite easy to see (and our test student saw on her own) that this pair of kicks should be equivalent to a kick along the diagonal in between them (Fig. 7a). This 'diagonal backward' kick is the correct way to negotiate a right angle turn. But it is extremely counter-intuitive without an analysis like the thought experiment above. Our

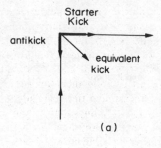

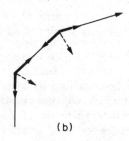

Fig. 7. Kick and antikick at a vertex combine to give 'central' equivalent kick.

test student had herself emphatically rejected it as a possibility when the diagonal backward kick was suggested to her before she had discovered antikicks.

One could easily imagine continuing the thought experiment with a turtle circle, a many-sided polygon, at each vertex giving an antikick back along the previous segment and a starter kick along the new segment. Combining those kicks in pairs gives a surprisingly clear and natural derivation of centripetal acceleration for circular motion (Fig. 7b).

In summary, the antikick story gives the following image for one mechanism, among many, for students learning in a computational environment:

(a) Students invent spontaneously (or we can ensure the reliability of this step with suggestions) ideas or concepts which though restricted in absolute terms, are both consonant with their intuitive dispositions and powerful in accomplishing what students wish to accomplish.

(b) After students gain confidence in the new idea, we can use it as leverage in increasing their level of understanding, if indeed it is necessary to intervene. With our sixth grade students, the short time they had available to play with dynaturtle did not give us evidence on whether, in general, students uniformly need help extending the antikick notion as envisioned above.

We caution physicist readers against regarding the above conceptual development in understanding such a 'simple' situation as trivial. Indeed, there is much evidence suggesting that such qualitative analysis is among the most difficult and latest developments, even in college students. For example, a recent study involving hundreds of students in several countries[6] shows that over 50% of students through the third year of university display tendencies to identify force and direction of motion similar to our elementary school students. In addition, I have documentation[7] of even bright M.I.T. students not only displaying similar problems as the elementary school students, but as well following similar developmental patterns in working out their difficulties, even after a year of high school and nearly a term of college physics!

CONCLUSION

It should be evident that our project has not aimed at developing curriculum to 'plug into' standard slots of school education. Although, for example, the orbit theory sketched above could well find a place in almost any conventional college physics course, we have aimed at the day, not quite at hand, when computation is not a scarce resource, when it is part of the background, the culture, as books and blackboards are today. In the summer high school program we have taught[1], students each have had at least two hours of available computer time *per day*, and some used much more. In the seminars we give to M.I.T. undergraduates the availability minimum is about three hours per week, and again we have had the luxury of allowing students who wished, considerably more.

At least as good an image for use of our 'products' is the growing home market for computers. We have already noticed the growth in awareness and aesthetics for dynamic computer games. Some of our dynaturtle students wished to start copying their favorite games; we expect they would have finished with much more elaborate versions, had time permitted. It happens that the current crop of home machines are much better suited to dynamics than to the detailed line drawings which characterizes turtle geometry, and if funding permits we intend to adapt our language and methods to take advantage of this situation. It may well be that the next generation of students will learn the essentials of Newtonian Mechanics via dynaturtle, or some variant, at home, leaving schools with the happy job of consolidating and extending that knowledge.

This is not to say we have no designs on schools. We have just completed a project thoroughly documenting the use of Logo in a conventional elementary school setting[5]. M.I.T. in collaboration with Texas Instruments and the Lamplighter School in Dallas, Texas, has undertaken an experiment to look at the possibilities for enhancing an elementary school environment generally if every child has his own computer to use for drawing, dynamic games, writing and editing, music, and whatever else the child or teacher can imagine. M.I.T. itself is also about to begin a rather large scale experiment in introducing the student-directed style I have been talking about in the freshman curriculum. The product will be a computer option of freshman physics and calculus which will offer students access to a great deal of computer power and computation- and exploration-oriented reformulations' of significant parts of the material.

REFERENCES

1. Abelson H. and diSessa A., Student Science Training Program in Math, Physics and Computer Science: Final Report to the NSF. MIT Logo Memo 26, MIT AI Memo 393, Massachusetts Institute of Technology Artificial Intelligence Laboratory, Cambridge, MA, (1976).
2. Abelson H. and diSessa A., *Turtle Geometry: The Computer as a Medium for Exploring Mathematics*. M.I.T. Press, In press.
3. Abelson H., diSessa A. and Rudolph L., Velocity Space and the Geometry of Planetary Orbits. *Am. J. Phys.* **43**, (1975).
4. diSessa A., ORBIT: A Mini-Environment for Exploring Orbital Mechanics: *Proceedings of the Second IFIP World Conference on Computers and Education*. (Marseille, France) North Holland Press (1975).
5. diSessa A., Papert S., Watt D. and Wier S., Final Technical Report to the National Science Foundation: Documentation and Assessment of·a Children's Computer Laboratory. M.I.T. LOGO Memos 52 and 53 (1979).
6. Viennot L., *La Raisonnment Spontané en Dynamique*. Hermann, Paris (1978).
7. diSessa A., *When Almost Everybody Does the Essentially Same Thing*: In preparation.
8. Papert S., *Mindstorms: Children Computers and Powerful Ideas*. Basic Books (Spring 1980).

INDEX